KHABAAR

FoodStory
Nina Mukerjee Furstenau,
series editor

KHABAAR

An Immigrant Journey
of Food, Memory, and Family

....

Madhushree Ghosh

UNIVERSITY OF IOWA PRESS, IOWA CITY

University of Iowa Press, Iowa City 52242
Copyright © 2022 by University of Iowa Press
uipress.uiowa.edu
Printed in the United States of America
Design by April Leidig

Printed on acid-free paper

Library of Congress Cataloging-in-Publication Data
Names: Ghosh, Madhushree, author.
Title: Khabaar: An Immigrant Journey of Food, Memory, and Family /
Madhushree Ghosh.
Description: Iowa City: University of Iowa Press, [2022] |
Series: FoodStory | Includes bibliographical references.
Identifiers: LCCN 2021045194 (print) | LCCN 2021045195 (ebook) |
ISBN 9781609388232 (paperback; acid-free paper) | ISBN 9781609388249 (ebook)
Subjects: LCSH: Cooking, Bengali. | Ghosh, Madhushree—Family. |
Scientists—United States—Biography. | East Indian American women—
Biography. | LCGFT: Cookbooks.
Classification: LCC TX724.5.I4 G474 2022 (print) | LCC TX724.5.I4 (ebook) |
DDC 641.595492—dc23
LC record available at https://lccn.loc.gov/2021045194
LC ebook record available at https://lccn.loc.gov/2021045195

Another world is not only possible, she's on her way.
Maybe many of us won't be here to greet her, but on a quiet day,
if I listen very carefully, I can hear her breathing.
—Arundhati Roy, "Come September,"
My Seditious Heart, 2019

For Baba and Ma—
ei je, etaa nao

CONTENTS

....

Khabaar tackles not only how immigrant food and South Asian food in particular traveled through colonization, migration, refugee journeys, and indenture; it is also about my childhood as the daughter of refugees and as an immigrant myself. While I pride myself in my memory, I am acutely aware that what I remember, or choose to remember, is what I want my world to adjust to. I have kept the names of most of the people in the essays as is and noted when I may be misremembering them. I have discussed with my surviving family members incidents that I am certain of, although they have sometimes remembered them very differently. I have stayed true to my recollection in *Khabaar* and am true to the "memory fades, memory adjusts" Didion school of thought.[1]

I have also called the neighborhood I grew up in Chittaranjan Park or C. R. Park—both have been used interchangeably. If you talk to anyone from there, whether they still live in that neighborhood or are elsewhere in the world, I can guarantee you they too will use both descriptors interchangeably.

The colonization of the mind and of our immigrant stories is a problematic minefield indeed. It takes decades for multilingual authors like myself to take a stance on how to present words that aren't English but that I grew up with. Should we italicize words our mothers raised us with or not? Are these words foreign, and if so, to whom? If a reader doesn't understand the word, what will they do? Stop reading? Start exploring? After all, isn't that what we do ourselves as writers, readers, and learners?

Why then, this italics-policing by many publishers to highlight an "exotic," "foreign," "unfamiliar" word? Read the sentence. Read the story. You'll get it. Or you'll ask.

It is easy for me to devolve into irrational rage. It's natural to internalize racism, sexism, even hatred, and descend into victimhood. I wrote *Khabaar* to understand what we question and what we track and how we follow the journeys of immigrant food stories. Jumoke Verissimo italicizes her Yoruba words to assert her selfhood through her writing, primarily because she learned English as a result of colonial legacy and education.[2] Khairani Barokka asked a question I myself have asked regularly: How normalized *is* italicizing words of our own languages, that it takes us years, if not decades, to unlearn?[3]

There have been multiple nudges to italicize Bengali and Hindi words in *Khabaar*. As a scientist by training, an immigrant by choice, and the daughter of refugees by destiny, to call myself one or the other feels like othering myself. Italics add another dimension to this exclusion. I can be one and the other. I choose not to italicize Bengali, Hindi, or other Indian language words. I hope you use or start to use them as liberally as I do here and in life. I do italicize *khabaar* because I want you to pay attention, not because it is foreign or simply because it's the book title.

In Bengali, we have twice as many vowels and consonants as the English alphabet. *S* is usually pronounced as "sh" and *s* has three distinct characters in the Bengali script. I've tried to keep the Bangla transliterations to as close to how we would pronounce it in my family—people who moved from Dhaka and Barisal to Kolkata, then New Delhi and now America through Partition and immigration.

This then brings us to the concept of food and its appropriation by white, English-speaking people. Imperialism—and as a result colonialism —has the dubious distinction of evangelizing spices and cuisines of colonized lands. I don't think we need to debate that. While Old World colonizers, such as the British, Spanish, Dutch, and Portuguese, currently have a significantly reduced influence, the New Order imperialists, such as the

United States and China, that have colonized Africa, Latin America, and parts of South Asia, are flourishing.

What does it mean when our lands are colonized? The stories are well known, but the impact over generations is felt through many layers. How are my ancestors connected to a Singapore kopitiam stall selling prata or a Durban restaurant selling lamb bunny chow? That story may be lost or, as it often happens in our cultures, passed down through oral lore, changing and morphing over the years.

Appropriation, however, especially of cuisines, remains constant. It seems that we're outraged daily about racist and toxic environments for BIPOC in food-focused companies, magazines, and media à la *Bon Appétit* and *New York Times* columnists.[4] Co-opting in a white-centric world re-inforces a white norm, a whitewashing of a food that has existed independently for centuries. While the topics are intertwined, to ignore privilege in India while talking about *khabaar* would be doing immigrant journeys a disservice.

Privilege in India comes through not only through colonization and our calculated association with those colonizers but also through wealth, which in turn is a result of class and caste. If we as South Asians and/or South Asian Americans don't acknowledge our societal status, which enables us to explore food journeys so easily or learn how lack of resources devastates lower castes and the casteless, we can't address what these food journeys truly inform.

Sharanya Deepak highlighted how food scarcity led Dalits—the untouchables, casteless people in the Hindu caste system—to create innovative cuisine.[5] When the "untouchables" are excluded from the Hindu caste system, denying them opportunities, foods, places of worship, and the right to equality, they improvise. Food tells the story of how middle-class families like mine separated the utensils used for the help from ours and ours from the guests who were given food on plates of the highest quality. I acknowledge my privilege. I learn to check it daily, and I work to unlearn every day.

I hope the journey you'll embark on with this book will spark a discussion about immigrants like me, how we came to be, what was done to us, how we love, and what our food illuminates. But more important, I hope *Khabaar* tells you about the land (and food) we left and still love dearly.

Finally, *Khabaar* wouldn't have been possible without the editors who helped champion, guide, and publish some of the essays that hold its essence. Sincere thanks to *Longreads* and Sari Botton for "Maachher Bazaar, Fish for Life," *The Juggernaut* and Snigdha Sur for "Peyaara Se Pyaar or the Love for Guava," Melissa Harrison Jameson and the editors at *The Kitchn* for "The Fast and Flavorful Spiced Lamb Curry That Pays Homage to My Mom," Donna Talarico-Beerman and the editors at *Hippocampus Magazine* for a version of "When Indira Died," and Dinty Moore at *Brevity* for another version of "Bole so Nihaal," parts of which are included in *Khabaar*. Editors are who keep writers going; we are just too awkward to say so.

Madhushree Ghosh
San Diego, 2021

KHABAAR

CHAPTER I

Peyaara se Pyaar or the
Love for Guava

Baba's tales of Dhaka were love stories. Stories of food—lullabies, poems, and odes to the mighty mango, the elegant okra (or lady fingers as we called them in our desh), or the shiny begun (eggplant). They were stories of a refugee who waited his whole life to return home while he made New Delhi his—and ours. Baba grew up when India hadn't been partitioned by the British into two countries, India and Pakistan. The two later became three: India, Pakistan, and Bangladesh. Desh for him was home. There, every fruit was fruitier, squash meatier, potatoes creamier. I didn't realize that for him homesickness was a yearning for a long-lost childhood home.

I didn't know the taan, the pull of the homeland then. I didn't appreciate what triggers memory in a refugee or immigrant's brain until I became an immigrant myself. The trigger, invariably, is food, whether it's the food you choose, the fruit you grow, or the fish you cook. Each dish—the smell, color, flavor, and taste—reminds us of a time when life was simpler, sweeter. Food comforts a need that connects us across borders and makes us believe we're still part of the land we left.

For me, the food that reminds me of home has always been the guava.

In 1976, when I was six, Baba's bank transferred him to New Delhi from a small town in Orissa. In that small town, we lived in a large bungalow. Even though it was a promotion, Baba moved our sleepy selves into a modest house in the fast-paced city. Rude, noisy, loud Delhi had no space to breathe. For us literary, music-loving Bengalis who loved food, talking, and singing, this place was hell. The Punjabis spoke roughly, the Haryanvis were crude, and the South Indians were too religious or too vegetarian (or both). We Bengalis eventually found our neighborhood. Named after Chittaranjan Das, a revered and long-dead freedom fighter, Chittaranjan Park had small green patches masquerading as parks. It was a slice of Kolkata in Delhi, a respite for Bengalis.

C. R. Park, as it is still known, was created when the newly established Indian government needed government officials, clerks, and office managers. Bengali refugees from what was then East Bengal moved into India, moved farther west to the capital for work, creating a neighborhood of educated, bourgeois refugees holding on to their Bengali sensibilities. Those Bengalis missed hilsa and rohu river fish, ridge gourds, bitter melon, and of course, shondesh. Right next to that neighborhood was Kalkaji, where Punjabi refugees from what's now Pakistan were grocery store owners or worked in car repair shops, gurudwaras, and small businesses. Two immigrant neighborhoods, two different sensibilities, two types of recollections of what used to be home.

. . . .

Our rented house in Chittaranjan Park had a wraparound garden, facing a huge living room with a kitchen on the side and extending to a vegetable garden patch overlooking old and retired neighbors. In this wraparound garden, Baba decided to grow vegetables and pretend this was home. That small patch was transformed into thin stalks of okra, squash blossoms, hot chili peppers, and bell peppers that Didi and I still call capsicum.

His usual lament?

"Bujhli toh, aamar deshe, in my land, everything was at least twice as large as here."

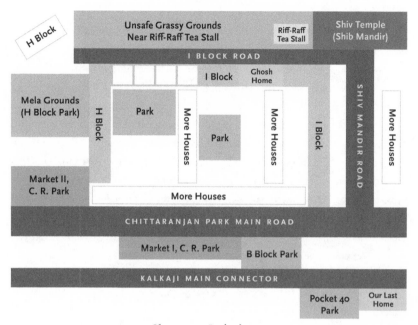

Chittaranjan Park schematic

. . . .

In 1993, when I boarded my first international flight, I sat at the window seat watching my country slowly dim into a whiff of clouds in the dark. I was headed to New York, the first daughter to leave for a PhD, the first Ghosh girl headed to America. The man sitting in the middle seat, a middle-aged Punjabi watching me cry into my handkerchief, asked, "Beta, first time to America?"

I nodded. I asked, "Where do you live in America?"

"Yuba City."

Seeing my confusion, he added, "We Punjabi farmers settled there decades ago. We grow all the produce. Us. And the Mexicans."

His hands holding his whiskey were tanned dark, his skin thick. The metal kara on his right wrist gleamed softly in the glow of the overhead light.

"You're American."

"Yes," he said proudly. "My grandfather married a Mexican when he moved to Yuba."

I rolled my eyes, disbelieving, but kept quiet—why question a stranger?

Later, at dinner, he helped me open the small butter packet since I had no idea which corner to pull the foil out from. It was a small rectangle, with Land O'Lakes emblazoned on it. A young Native American woman's face looked back, giving me butter obsequiously. A woman offering gifts, as if to earn friendship. In that moment, I felt I was that woman. Presenting gifts as if to earn a friendship. Later, much later, in 2020 the butter brand removed the "butter maiden" image after public outcry of how racist and stereotypical the image of a subservient Indian was. At that time in 1993, I was in awe that butter could fit in a package that small and that the packaging could be that secure.

"Here," he said, "look at this notch, very easy."

Pulling at the foil, his hands expertly separating it from the plastic, he added, "The butter is good, from Minnesota. You know Minnesota? Land of lakes, many lakes?"

Ignoring his question because I had no idea about Minnesota or lakes of any kind in America, I said, "Thank you," and dug into the butter.

It tasted like nothing. Air. Oil. Nothing. Amul butter—what I grew up on—now *that* was butter. The taste of sunshine, cow milk, churned whey, tinge of salt. The blue packaging, the yellow butter slabs wrapped in blue printed parchment paper. The butter melting in the Delhi summer. Ma used to cut the butter into slivers for daily use, swiftly transferring the rest into the butter slot in the top part of the door of our trusty refrigerator before it transformed into goop. The image on the package was the "Amul girl"—a precocious child in a poufy polka-dot dress with her hair partially up in a ponytail. A cartoon speech bubble saying, "Utterly butterly delicious!" and "Amul" in block letters above that, with "pasteurized" on the next line, "butter" on the next. Over the years the label has changed, the packaging's become spiffier, but the slogan remains. I've never been able to read "utterly butterly delicious!" without hearing the way the slogan was breathily and excitedly sung by a high-pitched jingle singer in Doordarshan ads on TV.

I tried to slather the Land O'Lakes butter on the rock-hard dinner roll. It was cold on the Thai Airways flight, and the butter never really melted. I put pieces of it on top of the bread like dew drops on a rock.

I never asked his name.

In my graduate school apartment in New York, I looked for Yuba City on a US map. It was very far away. It was also not a city. Not like New York.

. . . .

During the summer of 1977, Baba brought home three guavas from Dehradun, a hill station north of us. Fruit in Dehradun was exotic by Delhi standards—sweet lychees, juicy loquats, citrus fruits, mangoes, and guavas are what Dehradun was made of.

In Bengali, guavas are called peyaara. The Dehradun peyaaras Baba brought were dark avocado-skin green, not the usual yellow with brown spots. The inside was pinkish red with white seeds peeking out. We added a liberal sprinkling of salt and chili pepper to enhance the fruit's sweetness and slight tartness. Ma made aam sherbet with roasted unripe mangoes sweetened with molasses, spiced with roasted cumin, chili, and salt, blended in water. It wasn't strange to have fruit with a fruit drink then. It was hot and as a family, that's what we did on a summer day.

Combining Bengali and Hindi, Ma joked, "Peyaara se pyaar hua!" I'm in love with guava.

. . . .

After we ate the first batch of guavas together, only one guava remained. Maybe it was meant for Ma and Baba. Maybe they forgot. My brain fixated on the sole peyaara on the dining table, next to the watermelon and the dasheri mangoes. The peyaara needed to be eaten.

That afternoon, Didi and Ma were in their rooms—siesta time. To this day I swear the peyaara said, "Eat me. Eat me now."

A seven-year-old's hands are magically quiet when they need to be. I dared not look for the knife—it would be worse if fingers were sliced in the mission. I ate it whole. Guava juice trickled down my chin, onto my white kantha-stitch chemise. The seeds felt like crunchy dal moot, the savory chickpea flour snacks we had at 4 p.m. every day that summer with our Darjeeling tea. Still firm, the guava had a sweetness like no other. The red flesh in the center of the fruit glistened like Ma's lipstick. Every bite was a beauty. Every nibble was a joy.

Ma called out, "Rumjhum! Ki holo?"

As Bengalis, we all had our daak naam, the name our families used to call us with. One's formal name was for school admissions. Mine was Madhushree, a serious one, meaning the beauty of honey or the beauty of life. Baba called me Puchkey, or "little one." And the entire family—parents, cousins, uncles, aunts—called me Rumjhum. That was my daak naam. These days, those who call me that are few and far between.

"Ki holo?" Ma asked again.

"Nothing," I said, which meant Ma would get up to investigate. "Nothing" was code, meaning her girls were up to no good.

I had to get rid of the evidence. I threw the guava from the dining table area, through the open sliding door to the garden patch. I've played basketball and volleyball since then, but I've never had as accurate an aim as I did that summer of 1977.

Ma shuffled to the table.

I yelled, "I'm hungry."

Suspicious, she said, "You're never hungry."

Since I can't lie, I make my eyes go blank. Later, Didi would look high and low for the guava, complaining to both parents that I ate it. But my blank look conveyed innocence, and it saved me. Soon we forgot about the peyaara.

. . . .

In the United States, the Immigration Act of 1917 prevented Asians from becoming citizens.[1] The Sikh farmers, all male, in Yuba and Imperial Counties, in Northern and Southern California respectively, couldn't return to India because if they did, they wouldn't be permitted back into the United States. The 1913 California Alien Land Law prohibited them from owning land because they couldn't become citizens.

In 1850, California's anti-miscegenation law prevented whites from marrying blacks, Filipinos, and Asians.[2] The Sikh farmers couldn't go home to marry Indian women since they'd be unable to return to the country, and couldn't marry American women due to anti-miscegenation laws. As a result, the Sikh farmers began marrying Mexican women. About 378 marriages were performed in the early twentieth century between the Sikh farmers and Mexican women in the Central and Imperial Valleys of California, according to Karen Leonard,[3] University of California-Irvine. Of the nearly two thousand Sikh men, nearly 30 percent of them married Mexican women.

The farming men grew prune and peach trees—more than 60 percent of the produce in Yuba and Sutter Counties.

The guava, a Mexican fruit, is also grown in the plains of Punjab.

. . . .

India now produces about 45 percent of guavas globally.[4] The *psidium guajava*, or the common guava, is prevalent globally. In Brazil and other South American countries, the guava is a different species, *feijoa sellowiana*, commonly called feijoa—a thicker, smaller, dark green version. While guava grew wild in Latin America (it was found in archaeological sites in Peru that date to as early as 2500 BCE), it was introduced to India in the seventeenth century by the Portuguese colonizers. While not indigenous to the Indian subcontinent, India now produces most of the guava in the world—so many, in fact, that most Indians think the guava is theirs.

. . . .

Later that summer in 1977, after the guava incident, Baba pointed to a thin green stalk at the edge of the vegetable garden patch. Examining it with his fingers, he said, "This isn't a climber. It's a fruit tree. Hm."

"Hm," Didi and I repeated in unison.

By the next day, and also because I couldn't—cannot—keep a secret, I confessed to Didi that night, "That's my guava."

Instantly, she tattled, "Ma, Rumjhum did eat that last guava."

Baba turned from the young tall tree with a "Yes, shotti, Rumjhum, you grew a peyaara gaachh!"

I beamed like I had birthed that plant.

Ma, always the logical one, said, "That's a shame since we'll be gone before we get any fruit from it, eh?"

Baba sighed in resignation.

The tree grew, despite the concrete wall next to it.

Baba was promoted again. We left the wraparound garden house for a small town that we all hated. Bidding it goodbye, I promised the peyaara tree, "Aami abaar aashbo." I'll be back.

. . . .

In 1980, our family returned to Delhi, to another part of the neighborhood. When we visited the wraparound garden house, the tree was lush, peyaaras hanging from bent limbs. Of course, I stole a couple, how could I not?

Ma nodded in quiet appreciation. Baba said, "Let's see if it's red inside."

Yes, it was red, with pinkish seeds like little pearls. Sweet like no other. Our peyaara.

. . . .

Baba bumped into the new tenants of the wraparound house at the fish market in C. R. Park. He introduced himself, the most extroverted man I've ever known, and he regaled them with stories of the tree and his daughter.

He also noted, as if casually, "The tree has too much fruit, no? What do you do with them?"

Those sweet gullible people said, "Too many guavas. This tree has so much fruit, do you want them?"

. . . .

With my peyaara, Ma made guava jelly. Hanging the fruit pulp in a muslin cloth for hours, she placed a dish under it to catch the juice. Stirring the thick juice with grated ginger, red chili peppers, and ground pepper, she thickened it with molasses, slow cooking the juice and pulp—my childhood was the smell of guavas, sticky with natural pectin. The next morning, she served it with toast, as if we lived off the land in this metropolitan city.

....

A little over a decade later, after I moved to America in the early 2000s, Baba died—that large heart couldn't last through decades of chain-smoking. Three years later, Ma followed, felled by a broken heart. They lived and died in the mini-Bengal neighborhood in Delhi, having given up on ever returning to Bangladesh.

The day after Ma's shraddha, I went for a walk in my old neighborhood. My then husband wanted to show me a park he'd discovered. We headed past Market No. 1, up toward Shiv temple (Shib mandir in Bengali).

"We're getting closer to the wraparound garden house," I said. "Our house is just around the corner. My peyaara tree."

The house looked smaller, now painted gray with gaudy magenta trim.

"I threw a guava in that corner, and it turned into a tree. Ma made jelly from it." I pointed.

But the tree, which would have been almost as old as I was, was gone. The roots had given up, given in.

"I guess there's no jelly to make, is there?" he said.

At that time, I thought he was being unkind on purpose. Later, I realized he wasn't, he was stating the obvious. There was no jelly to make, the tree was gone.

When I returned back to the house Baba had died in, Didi was in the kitchen.

I told her, "The peyaara gaachh is gone."

Her eyes were blank, hiding the pain well, as she nodded silently.

The Ghoshes have never been very good at showing emotion. I remember her eyes focused on the daal she was boiling on Ma's stove, as if nothing else existed that day.

. . . .

In San Diego, where I live these days, Mexican fruits remind me of home. Some of the smaller mangoes look like dasheri—small, yellow, exploding with flavor. Custard apples are differently shaped from the aata with which I grew up. In Spanish, they're called "aate," very similar to Bengali.

Goya guava jelly sells for $3.99 at any grocery store near Old Town San Diego, where Mexicans and colonizers coexisted. This guava jelly features the fruit pulp along with red coloring, preservatives, and complicated sugars I can't pronounce. It may not be Ma's jelly, but guava it is.

One doesn't really know where we grow our own roots. I wonder if Baba thought that his garden would outlast him in that wraparound garden house. Or did he grow the trees and plants, knowing that one day they too would be gone?

. . . .

I live in a house close to where white settlers took over Mexican and Native American land. Three hours east of me is the Imperial Valley, where Sikh farmers sought Mexican farmworkers as wives. Marriages now occur outside the community, with few remaining traces of that group. My own immigrant roots are loose and unmoored, mostly. But sometimes a green stalk rises next to a concrete wall when most unexpected. And reminds me of a country that was as sweet as the guava I stole.

CHAPTER 2

Maachher Bazaar,
Fish for Life

It's been more than a decade since my parents left. I still don't say they
died, because they didn't. Not to me. All my American friends whose
parents are still alive console me, "It'll get easier, Madhu," shortening
my name with the casual authority most non-Indians have, "it'll get easier
with time."

I have been waiting for that ease for years now.

When I moved to America over a quarter of a century ago, what hit me
wasn't what I saw but what was absent on the streets, in neighborhoods,
near the ocean, in movie theaters, in parks. The absence of older people.
Everywhere, there were only young families, young singles, children, and
animals. Lots of well-dressed puppies and even more tottering, unbalanced
children. The older generation was hidden in assisted living buildings behind decrepit malls, in high-rises facing lakes for exorbitant rental prices,
or in Florida around golf courses.

In 1993, I used to tell Baba when I'd call home every other weekend
for fifteen minutes at $2.05 per minute on an MCI calling card: "It's as if
they are afraid of seeing old people, Baba. Like that reminds Americans of
impending death."

I had arrived in America that fall, with two suitcases and a few hundred
dollars in travelers' checks. In 1993, I was invincible, young, and convinced

that Baba would live forever. We could discuss the Americanness of this life without worrying that death would ever reach us.

Baba would reply, laughing, "Ah, but it's more than death, though. The previous generation guides the newest generation. The stories pass from the previous generation not to their children but their grandchildren. The white people seem to have forgotten that—shotti, such a shame."

I laughed with him, our favorite pastime, rolling our eyes at the follies of "these Americans."

. . . .

I was six in '76 when we lived in I Block in C. R. Park in South Delhi.[1] The house number was 1612. We Ghoshes have always referred to that rental house as sholosho baaro—1612—our house number. In '76, the neighborhood was quiet, sparsely populated. By nightfall, when nervous Bengalis headed home from work, thugs, robbers, and dacoits from the nearby states of Punjab and Haryana drove by in search of weary travelers and nervous Bengalis returning home from work. As the Delhi winter descended, Ma, Didi, and I locked the sliding doors, turned off all the front room lights, and waited for Baba to return from work at the bank. Every other minute, Ma got up, peered outside, straining against the dim streetlight, watching for untoward movement, for Baba. Untoward movement could be a leaf moving, a tomcat climbing roofs, or birds squawking in trees; it was never a lurking bandit. Yet Ma scrutinized each movement. And each movement outside the curtain was deemed suspect.

Each time Ma turned from the window, she said, "He's late again."

Even though Baba never returned before eight, Ma always waited from 6 p.m. onward and claimed he was late. So every evening, Didi and I sat at the table, homework almost complete, waiting for Baba to return for two hours, because that was Ma's routine. We did what Ma did.

Baba returned, singing a long-forgotten Bengali song, and we heard him in the Delhi fog before he opened the gate. I, the daughter who should have been the son—the one on whose birth her ma wept with disappointment

Fish curry

that the Ghoshes were cursed with another girl—I rushed to open the sliding door.

"Baba, Baba, Baba!"

There wasn't much to say. We aren't, weren't, a demonstrative family. We never jumped into our father's arms or hugged our mother. We grinned at each other. That was enough. That is enough.

"Yes, Puchkey, I can hear you," Baba said every day. He called me Puchkey, the little one. I was after all, the littlest of all the cousins in the larger Ghosh family.

Decades later, when I returned and all the cousins were wizened, I was still Puchkey, my nickname, the name the family connected me to. Even now, I have to stop myself from introducing myself as the little one. Even now, when I am almost the only one remaining.

"Yes, Puchkey, I can hear you."

Ma followed me outside, hands outstretched. Baba handed her the newspaper-wrapped parcel, not his heavy briefcase. The *Statesman*, a newspaper every Bengali reads, was what wrapped around the parcel. Ma didn't ask if the pickpockets, thieves, or dacoits from the villages of Haryana were on the streets, nor did she ask how his day went or how the traffic was. All she asked was what mattered.

"Ki aanle," she asked, "What did you bring this time?"

Grinning, his eyes crinkling behind his glasses, Baba said, "Surprise, Sila, surprise."

I yelled at Didi, "Come, come, look, Baba brought us a surprise."

Didi, three years older than me in age, decades in soul, walked to the package, stuck her nose close in, and announced, "Yech! Puchkey, it's fish again."

"It's a surprise fish, Didi."

Rolling her eyes, she continued, "Really? When you open it, will it stare at us with big eyes and will it yell, 'Surprise!'?"

I shoved her with the fish package so that she squealed like the girl that she was. To this day, Didi doesn't touch fish.

. . . .

There is a daringly mischievous laugh in author Samin Nosrat's eyes when she goads us to taste something in *Salt, Fat, Acid, Heat*.[2] Her curly hair, her full cheeks, her dark eyes—if Baba were still alive, he would have said, "Oi meye ta Bangali." That girl is Bengali. Even though Nosrat is very obviously Persian-American.

To call someone Bengali was the ultimate praise from Baba—that meant she belongs to us, that she's instantly accepted as ours. Her recipes are simple, straightforward, and scientific. What's not to love?

And add to that, she always wanted to write. She was creative, a starving poet, in college. A cook, a chef, and an author. All Bengali things—given that Bengal has given the world literature that has won Nobel Prizes, Tagore, Rabindra sangeet, music that other Indian regions emulate, and a cuisine so fresh, fragrant, and colorful that every Bengali can wax eloquent about food from home, desi khabaar. Even in America, every Bengali I've met will steer conversations to food, cooking, eating, music, occasionally politics, and often literature. Samin's excitement while discovering new recipes, old traditions and conversations seems Bengali to me, and I am sure it would have been to Baba if he'd met her. What's not to love?

. . . .

Ma was already in the kitchen, chopping onions, a few garlic cloves. The lentils were in the pressure cooker, simmering in cumin and turmeric.

Ma smiled at me. "You know what to do, don't you, dear?"

I placed the newspapers on the floor, jumping from one foot to the other in anticipation. I knew what was to happen next, and I couldn't wait. Baba returned from the bathroom, changed into comfortable pajamas and shirt, singing yet another Rabindra sangeet, stopping when he forgot the lyrics.

"Sila," he said, "This time I got rohu."

"The whole, whole fish," Ma exclaimed. "That's too much, how will we finish it, what's wrong with—"

But her anger melted when Baba smiled at her. That's how they always stopped their arguments. No one denied my father's charm; even when he bought too many fish, his wife found him irresistible but would never confess to that.

. . . .

People gravitate to Samin's laugh. People of color are attracted to her because she—the daughter of immigrants—is the Great Hope. People identify with her otherness. And then, people are relieved when her otherness doesn't agitate them. She is a safe outsider who's really an insider. She's also young, relatively privileged, brought up in Southern California, in the city adjacent to the one I now call home, in an upper-middle-class household. Samin isn't threatening. Samin was able to save enough to go to Chez Panisse for a high-end dinner with her then college boyfriend. It is a life of privilege when a nineteen-year-old is able to afford a high-end restaurant. Most of us at nineteen couldn't have imagined saving even half that, no matter how many jobs we held to do so. But it was that dinner that opened her eyes to the world of cooking. That in turn, led to her working in the world-famous restaurant run by Alice Waters, queen of the sustainable slow food revolution.

Come to think of it, most cooks and chefs of color don't have the privilege of saving to splurge on a high-end dinner in Berkeley. Samin may be an outsider, but outsiders have privilege too—privilege she's acutely aware of, to the point that she uses her spectacular fame abundantly to highlight others of color not as fortunate. As she's said on multiple talk shows, "My heroes . . . some of these people are in the back kitchen behind the scenes (and not on camera)."[3]

It's her infectious giggle that attracts us, despite the privilege. Her laugh makes us relax. Samin's story remains that of love, hard work, and immigrant success. She doesn't make her difference a discomfort.

. . . .

The boti, a curved knife attached to a wooden stand, was placed in the center of the newspapers I had arranged on the floor. Patience was never my virtue, and at six, less so.

"Baba, Baba, Baba!"

"Puchkey, coming, uff!"

That wintry night in 1976, I learned about fish and what it meant to us. Baba sat down on the piri, a little stool, held the boti between his big and second toe, and held his hand out for the rohu. Ma turned on the lights so he could see clearly and lifted the fish from the sink, ran more water over it, and then handed it to him.

"Stay away, Puchkey, it's very sharp."

"Looks heavy, Baba."

"Help me lift it, Puchkey."

He brought the head closer to the blade, and I held the tail. This was important work, and I had the apprentice's role.

He said, "Look, the head, then the body, the top part is meaty, red, puffy. The bottom part, before the tail, has a hole running through. Do you know what's in the hole?"

"Food, right?"

"Yes, what the fish ate. We want to eat the fish, not what the fish ate, got it?"

"Yes, Baba."

He asked me to hold the tail at an angle. "It cuts easier if we hold it that way," he said.

"What angle is it?" he asked.

"Obtuse, Baba?"

He nodded; his daughter wasn't a bad student at all. "My mother taught me," he said.

"About obtuse angles?"

He laughed at my childish assumption and explained, "How to cut fish. Clean the guts, cut the fish."

I listened, carefully, each word of his imprinting in me.

"Know what's yours and eat that—not what the fish ate, but the fish. That's life for Bengalis—you eat fresh, you live fresh, you live life."

Entering the kitchen, Ma heard the tail end of our conversation. She interjected, a smile in her voice, "What are you teaching my daughter now, huh?"

"We absorb the fish's life. We live because they did," Baba said. He was serious. "Never forget, Puchkey, fresh fish. For fresh life. Always."

Baba left to wash his hands. I watched Ma fry the onions in mustard oil. The slices sizzled and the pungent steam stung my eyes, but I was riveted. She added black onion seeds and a paste of turmeric, cumin, ginger, and red chili powder. She stirred it, pushing me away from the gas stove if I got too close. My head just barely reached the counter, and mostly I saw her drop the fish and heard the sizzle of each piece cooking in the spices.

"What do you want to be, Puchkey? Fish cutter or fish cook?"

"Fish eater!"

She laughed and added water to the curry, lowered the flame, covering the koraai. The house smelled of onions and garlic. My stomach growled. She bent down and pinched my still chubby cheeks.

"Hungry, are you, my little girl?"

. . . .

The basic concept of salt, acid, fat, and heat isn't new, nor is it novel. In Western culture, where sweet plays an unnecessary central role, Samin defends the four essential elements as what's needed in any type of cuisine. Sweet-sour or sweet-spicy are hints to the sweetness of any dessert or savory dish. But the four elements are global—salt, acid, fat, and heat.

. . . .

That night, Ma tucked me into bed. Didi flopped about next to me, half-asleep. Ma left to tie her long hair before bed. Baba stepped in and tucked the thick quilt around his girls.

He stage-whispered: "Puchkey, Puchkey . . ."

"Don't bother her, ogo," Ma called out, but he continued anyway.

"Be ready tomorrow evening. Seven. We're going on an adventure."

"Where, Baba?"

"Maachher bazaar. The fish market."

Ma was at the door, her fingers twisting her hair into a thick plait. "Turning her into a boy, are you, eh?"

He smiled.

I couldn't sleep that night.

. . . .

Baba wasn't very reliable, nor was he punctual, usually. But this time, he was. I was ready in my new red wool coat, thick wool black tights, and two sweaters underneath. He dropped his briefcase, Ma handed him his tea, and he slurped it quickly. Holding out his big hand he said, "C'mon!"

I held it tight and caressed the square steel ring on his middle finger, the one his mother gave him before she died.

I waved at Didi, "It's an adventure! Bye!"

She stuck her tongue out.

Ma fussed over my wool cap and tightened it over my ears. Baba and I headed to the Chittaranjan Park fish market in the dark. He held a large flashlight, swinging it in front so we didn't trip over the sleeping street dogs. This adventure was ours. We walked in silence, accompanied by my excited heart beating kadunkakadunkakadunka.

"Are there a lot of fish, Baba?"

"Yes, the river ones and the ocean ones."

"Like rohu?" I said, knowing this name, one of our favorite river fish.

Nodding he said, "Hilsa, koi, magur, the fish with whiskers, and chondona, the pretend hilsa . . ."

"How do you find out which one's hilsa and which one's chondona?"

"Practice, daughter, practice." He let go of my hand and slapped both of his against the flashlight, like he was squishing the beam.

"The chondona fish's body is flat, cheptaa. Chondona flat, hilsa not; chondona flat, hilsa not . . ."

I ran to catch up, the rhythm of our feet echoing in the dark. Chondona flat, hilsa not, I kept repeating to myself with each step. That's how I learned about fish.

. . . .

Samin grew up in La Jolla, next to the Pacific Ocean, a daughter of immigrant Iranian parents, eating Persian food. She did not start cooking seriously till she reached college.

"Grilled cheese sandwiches were my thing," she says, grinning ear to ear, unapologetic. She was an English major, poetry was her jam.

Sometimes, a dinner is all it takes to change the course of one's passion. Samin's journey changed at Chez Panisse, when she was nineteen.

. . . .

We neared the fish market. The lights were brighter. The Delhi Transport Corporation buses zipped past on Main Street. Passengers jumped off running vehicles, and the fishermen outshouted each other attracting their customers, "Magurmagurmagurmagurmagurmagur! C'mon sir! Fresh fish, just off the truck this evening!"

"Don't look at his stinky fish—here, sir, good pabda, only twenty rupees a kilo! Ghosh sir, sir, come on, here!"

"Arrey, Ghosh sahib, how was the rohu? Wife liked it, right?"

The fisherman who sold the rohu smiled, flashing his red paan-stained teeth at us. Dark-skinned, as most fishermen at the market are, his old genji vest covered the knot of the striped lungi that covered his legs and expanding waist. On his wrist, a silver amulet; on his right ear, a ring.

"Fishermen class," Baba bent down to whisper in my ear. "He's from a generation of fish people."

"Ki, your daughter, sahib?" the fisherman enquired.

"Yes, Bhimu," my father said, putting his hand on my head. I let him, even though his hand was so heavy I felt my neck collapse. That was one of the few times my father's hand touched my head with pride that I was a Ghosh, his girl.

"Besh, besh," Bhimu nodded, pointing at the pabda. The thin silvery fish lay on the sloping cemented table in front of him, all faced left, like Muslims facing Mecca. Or that's what I thought. Bhimu scooped water from a dirty green mug, splashing them. They seemed to jump in surprise.

"See, sahib? They are still alive. See? So fresh!"

Baba bent down to examine more closely. He pulled me forward. I hesitated.

He asked softly, "How will you learn otherwise?"

Between the table and us was a naalaa, an open gutter to let the fish guts and water pass by without spreading all over the path. I stood at the edge, careful I didn't slip into the fishy moat. The place smelled of fish, sweat, and the chicken in coops across the aisle near the Muslim butcher's shop.

Bhimu picked up an eight-inch pabda, "Look, Didi. "He called me elder

sister, even though he was gray-haired and probably older than Baba—
"fresh fish smell. It can't get any better."

Baba raised his hand. "Two kilos. Twenty rupees for two, no bargaining."

Bhimu rolled his eyes, raised his hands up to the sky. "Oh, sahib, how will I feed my children? This is robbery, Ghosh sahib!"

"Dhur, Bhimu! Stop. If you don't give this fish to my daughter for twenty, then I know you can feed your children the same fish. So, you decide."

This went on for minutes. Tired, I tugged at Baba's hand. He ignored me. Bargaining and Bengalis are like twins. One can't exist without the other.

Bhimu finally agreed to twenty-five. Baba sighed as if he was doing Bhimu a favor. Bhimu pulled up a scale, like the justice scales at the government courthouse near Connaught Place. Only his scale was rusty, and in addition to the weights, he placed extra knobs of metal pieces to level the balance.

Baba watched the fish land on the scale, a hawk eyeing his food. "Stop, enough!" he said, when Bhimu added yet another pabda.

"What, Ghosh Sahib, only ten? Who can feed the family with only ten?"

Baba waved, "Clean it, will you?"

Bhimu pulled out his boti. The blade was five times longer than the one at home. Each time he removed the whiskers, the tail, the fins, the blade sang.

Baba pointed to the bhetki next to the pabda, "Here, look at the gills."

He pulled the head and the flap up.

"The gills are red. It was breathing when captured. The blood was flowing—"

"So?"

"Look in the lantern light. The blood is still liquid."

"Of course, Baba, blood is liquid, what else will it be?"

He shook his head, no. "If the fish were old, the gills would be sticky. The blood would congeal. You need to know, Puchkey, that's how you select good fish. Check the eyes."

"Eyes?"

"Yes, there should be no red or yellow in them. That means it's fresh. Check the fish scales."

"Scales, why?"

"If they are flaky and come off, even before the fish touches the boti, then the fish is old, losing its oil."

"Gills cannot be gummy, right?"

"You're learning."

Money and fish changed hands. Bhimu said, "Salaam, Didi, come again."

I waved back.

Baba carried the fish in the newspaper back home. On the way in the dark, I held the flashlight to show him the way.

With each step, he sang, "Aami cheeni go cheeni tomaare, ogo bideshini. Tumi thaako shindhu paarey, ogo bideshini."

I recognize you, oh stranger to these lands. You may live oceans away, oh stranger to these lands.

Ma opened the door, a small smile on her lips, "What did you bring, Puchkey?"

I grinned back at her.

. . . .

Almost three decades have passed since that night. We moved from that house in I Block to the house Baba built for Ma across from Market No. 1—we, creatures of habit that most Bengalis are, stayed in the same neighborhood, among Bengalis. The food remained the same, the prices increased exponentially.

Didi and I left for America, I for graduate school, seven years before her. She moved to the East Coast and I to San Diego. Two ends of an enormously large country. Now, as it was then, Didi still doesn't touch fish, while the fish I cook is from organic supermarkets, sustainable, free of chemicals. I have no idea whether they are river or ocean fish. I don't know the fishermen who caught the bass or the tilapia.

We returned home every other year, the annual and biannual treks of immigrants who believe they will return for good in the future. But that future doesn't show up.

....

Samin's mast-o-khiar recipe in the *New York Times* isn't hers or her own creation.[4] It's a staple on every Iranian dinner table, as she so rightly points out. In Persian, khiar is cucumber. In Hindi, it's kheera. Mast-o-khiar translates directly as yogurt and cucumber.

Bengalis usually cook with yogurt but don't consume it as a side dish. They may sweeten it with molasses or jaggery to eat as dessert, mishti doi (sweet yogurt).

I learnt the North Indian way to eat and cook with yogurt when we moved to New Delhi. It was where summers were hot and dry, dishes were spicy and needed yogurt to cool down the fire of ginger-garlic combinations in vegetable curries or slow-cooked meat dishes. Raita is what North Indians call their yogurt side dishes. Hands down, mast-o-khiar has a substantially heftier flavor than raita, along with a handful of walnuts and sweet pomegranate seeds for crunch and balance.

....

2004. I got the call that every daughter dreads when she lives in America and her parents are back home. This time, the flight was a blur, the announcements garbled, and when I landed, I craned my neck at the arrivals gate, just in case I could spot Baba's wool cap and his twinkling eyes behind his glasses—him searching for me as I was for him. Just in case. But he won't be waiting for me at that gate ever again. Instead, this was a visit to cremate my father.

....

The daughters are to stay at home. The wife, more so. The dead are never accompanied to the cremation grounds by women. We aren't allowed—according to religion, women are "unclean." It is simply not done.

And so, we went to the cremation grounds—Ma and her daughters—to cremate our father, her husband. I took Ma's hand and guided her from our house. The cousins, the men, looked on, grief stricken, but now in shock that their aunt and their cousins, women all, were headed to the shamshan ghat to give mukhagni, lighting the fire to the mouth of the deceased.

He looked asleep when we brought him to Lodi Garden cremation grounds. Didi and I went in to help my mother light the funeral pyre where her husband of over four decades lay. The priest shook his head in disapproval. Baba, felled by an attack to his heart. He seemed like an old man in his kurta and dhoti that we wrapped around him. We sprinkled Dolce & Gabbana—or was it Brut?—on his cheeks, a fragrance he loved. Ma couldn't walk fast, arthritis reminding us of her mortality. Her half-blind eyes kept wandering, as if looking for Baba everywhere but where he was—lying right in front of us.

Baba, the honest, upright banker, was cremated first. He was first in line because we bribed the priests. The irony of this wasn't lost on us, but we ignored it. My honest Baba wouldn't have approved. But cremation is something we needed to do right away. He had already waited two days for his daughters to return home.

The priest gave Ma a stack of incense sticks. "Mrs. Ghosh, place them on your husband's chest, his feet."

He sprinkled ghee and prayers over Baba, who was covered with a soft cotton cloth, flowers, marigold, rose petals sprinkled over him like he was a meadow. He didn't look like himself, Baba, so it didn't register that it was the last time I'd see him.

Didi and I helped Ma light the pyre. Agnostics at heart, Didi and I, we let Ma dictate to us how she'd say farewell to her husband. Her purple sari, with a gold zari border, shone dully when she dropped the last incense stick on Baba's chest. Her cries were soft, her eyes confused. We howled with her, as the floor underneath the wooden pyre where Baba lay moved. The rails were like train tracks. The rumbling ahead made it seem as if Baba was headed to the next station. In the far corner, the fire wall opened with a whoosh of air, carbon, and heat. Baba moved along the rails. We couldn't stop it. We couldn't stop him.

"Baba, Baba," I cried, for no reason, and when I looked at Didi, she was calling out to him too. This was too quick. This was too soon. He was gone, and we had Ma between us.

. . . .

We are the agnostics. But we had a mother who believed in tradition—the right way to bid farewell to her husband. Didi and I complied, silent. We took her to the temple; we invited all their friends and family members to witness the pinda daan ceremony. The card was white, the lettering in black:

We, the bereaved daughters of S. N. Ghosh along with his bereaved wife, S. Ghosh, respectfully ask you to join us in the Shraddha ceremony in Shiv Temple, Chittaranjan Park.

That morning of the shraddha ceremony was bright, the early winter Delhi sun strong, as if by mistake. The air still smelled of the smoke from the dhunuchis used to fete Durga in her festival when she came down from the heavens to her father's home on earth. Durga was long gone, her straw, clay, and enamel-paint sculpture immersed in the Yamuna River by the young devotees and volunteers of the Chittaranjan Park Puja Committee.

We arrived early at the temple. It used to be a one-room Shib mandir. When we had just moved into the neighborhood in 1976, Didi and I used to walk from our I Block home, my hand held tightly in hers, up the uneven steps to the temple. Across the road, on the corner, was our home. Ma waited for us there, craning her neck, watching for us, and she would wave, wave. Back then, we'd wave back before walking back together again, Didi's hand holding mine tightly still.

That same Shib mandir was now three buildings, with marble donation plaques as tiny steps along the pathway—gifts from nonresident Indians, living outside the country in America, England, the Middle East, or elsewhere—donations with gold engravings noting each marble plaque as a gift in honor of their dead mother or father or both while also noting that it represents a cash donation from San Francisco or Dubai or someplace "foreign." The path was lined with expensive evergreen plants gasping for breath in the Delhi heat, also representing cash donations from similar nonresident Indians, assuaging their guilt for leaving their birth country and their parents with meaningless donations like these wilting palms, ferns, and rose bushes. Heading to the first temple, we helped Ma into a chair. She couldn't sit cross-legged anymore. Arthritis was killing the body slowly, painfully, but her mind, still agile, could only watch helplessly.

The priest chanted my father's name, asked Ma for his ancestors' names, caste, and lineage. Ma provided them, her schoolteacher memory on auto-pilot, her eyes now permanently swimming in tears.

Baba didn't like pretend shows like these ceremonies. But I was sure he'd be appreciative of his family taking part in this event together, in the same neighborhood we had moved to as children. Didi and I, the bereaved daughters, standing at the gate, gave each well-wisher a packet of shondesh, a savory, a roshogolla, and a thank you for coming to pay respects.

. . . .

Samin's ten Persian recipes in the *New York Times* are simple ones that look like they took forever to make. They have been simplified for Western home cooks but still hold the flavor that's distinctly Persian.

The immigrant cooking that Samin experienced was really what she got at home. Her mother showed her how to miss a country through food. She writes, "My mom, who left Iran in 1976, steeped us in the smells, tastes, and traditions of Persian cuisine. . . . She taught us that regardless of what was going on in the news, home is home, and nothing can transport you there like taste."[5]

. . . .

Eleven days after Baba left, we held the niyam bhongo ceremony, the breaking of the mourning period rituals with careful consideration to all who mourned with the grieving family. We invited the men who'd helped take

Baba to the crematorium, the women who'd helped Ma repeat every minute of the last moments of Baba's life, over and over till the words no longer held any grief for Ma.

We cooked Baba's favorite foods. Baba didn't like his desserts contaminated by North Indian additives like rose essence, so we made his roshogollas with sugar water only. We slowly cooked cholaar daal with coconut bits, cinnamon, and chickpeas; cauliflower curry with cumin and green peas; mishti doi, using only the best jaggery from West Bengal. Someone brought in fresh fish—I no longer remember who. Didi cooked it with mustard paste and green chilies in Baba's memory. Didi didn't touch the fish with her bare hands but awkwardly poked it with a fork, layering one spice over the other gingerly. I watched. I couldn't grieve. I didn't repeat the story of the phone call I received in San Diego, telling me Baba was gone. I didn't repeat it to anyone. I held my grief, pretended to be fine, and watched Didi prepare the fish.

Two weeks later, Didi headed back to the East Coast, her visa and her husband's job preventing the luxury of mourning longer in India with us. I was left with Ma, in the cold November wintry night. I had a green card by then, which gave me the freedom to stay, knowing I could leave whenever I wanted to. And I didn't want to.

I called up my work, told them I was on family medical leave. They reluctantly said sure, Madhu, stay with your mother. Underneath that professional concern, I could feel unsaid words: Madhu, don't be so emotional. It's only your father. Everyone's parents die. The professional email from my manager, cc'ed to HR, was almost sympathetic, but it was the uncomfortable response of an American used to assisted living homes tucked behind malls and office fronts, of someone unused to being reminded of death and dying. I glanced at it, noted that the leave was granted, per US law, and shut my email down. I had Ma to take care of.

C. R. Park in 2004 had transformed into a well-lit metropolitan neighborhood. Durga Puja festivities had dimmed a month before. The only thieves in the neighborhood were likely shifty folks stealing cable lines from the main street shops to access the latest Bollywood channels for free. Baba's songs were missing. Soon the well-wishers stopped visiting, the neighbors stopped nosing around. Soon it was only Ma and me in the house Baba built for us.

. . . .

Ma's tears became her constant companion. She sat in front of the portable heater, warming her frozen arthritic feet near the red-hot heating coil, hunched beyond her sixty-eight years, staring unseeing at the rod, half-blind, waiting for Baba's footsteps, heavy, one step after another, waiting for Baba's voice, singing a line of a long-forgotten song, one step, one step up to our floor of our three-level home . . . waiting, waiting, waiting. But he didn't climb the stairs, nor did he sing, "I recognize you, oh stranger, you come from oceans far away."

I told her, "It's evening, Ma, drink some tea."

"Where to, Puchkey?" she asked.

"I'm going to the fish market. Could you ask the maid to grate some chilies with ginger?"

. . . .

Samin's mast-o-khiar uses labneh, or the sourest thick yogurt one can find. Add in walnuts, raisins, pomegranate seeds, but mostly herbs—dill, cilantro, mint, parsley, or tarragon in copious amounts—and cucumber (diced) to make this yogurt dish sing. Grated garlic is mixed into the thick yogurt and, to make it less watery, diced cucumber is added just before serving. Concentrated yogurt starter bacterial cultures containing *Staphylococcus thermophilus* and *Lactobacillus bulgaricus* make labneh rich in probiotics and a godsend for our gut.[6]

Even though she tells us that salt, acid, fat, and heat are key in every dish, the sugar in golden raisins and pomegranate seeds makes her mast-o-khiar ever so Persian, irresistible with a hint of surprising sweetness.

Samin's rise is revered as the rise of immigrant hope—hope for the women in the back kitchens, the ones of color, of different countries, of other languages. Her relatability, her obvious immigrant-daughter status, her very confidence of who she is are a joy to watch as she navigates the world of words and food in a reality-televised world.

....

That evening, I didn't need a flashlight. The streetlamps were fluorescent-bright. People walked without fear of pickpockets as if it were daytime. Video parlors with Abhishek Bachchan and Rani Mukherjee posters adorned the main street shops. Big buses hurtled past. The market crowd ballooned like monsoon clouds. Bengalis—now flashier, louder, wearing foreign watches, expensive saris, designer jeans—walked through the market, mobile phones in hand.

The fish market was still in the corner. The concrete floors were glazed, permanent-looking. The naalaa that in 1976 was made of mud was now permanent, covered so no one stepped on fish guts. The fishermen wore T-shirts with slogans of Just Do It and All Iz Well. Instead of lungis, they wore shorts, polyester, hibiscus-printed Hawaiian knockoffs. In the corner, a wrinkled fisherman, the only one in a lungi and an old gray shirt, looked at me but didn't beckon me to see his fish. His silence made me approach him. The silver amulet on his wrist winked at me.

"Ki, Didi?" Bhimu said, his eyes twinkling. "It's been a while, na?"

I pretended not to recognize him. "Koto?" I asked, pointing at the bhetki.

"Your father taught you well, Didi. He taught you about fish . . ."

I gave in. "Yes, it's been a while, Bhimu," I said.

I opened the gills with my fingers. They fanned out like the pink lizards of Jurassic Park. I wiped my hands on the alcohol-wipe Bhimu offered me.

"All foreign-return children want these wipes," he explained when I thanked him.

Baba taught me well. Fresh fish, fresh life.

So, I said, "Now tell me how fresh is this bhetki? How much per kilo? Don't you try to cheat me, I know your wily ways!"

My raita is also a bastardized version of what I ate in New Delhi decades ago. In San Diego, I use thick kefir instead of homemade yogurt. Probiotic bacteria in kefir are an alphabet soup: *Lactobacillus acidophilus, Bifidobacterium bifidum, Lactobacillus delbrueckii subsp. bulgaricus, Lactobacillus helveticus, Lactobacillus kefiranofaciens, Lactococcus lactis,* and *Streptococcus thermophilus.* The science behind enabling the microbiome to flourish isn't lost on me. Nor is the scientific basis of Bengali cuisine, a combination of protein; anti-inflammatory ginger, garlic; antibacterial turmeric; appetite-inducing / acid-reducing green and red chili paste as well as garam masala (home ground)—a miracle ratio of cumin, coriander, nutmeg, ginger, and anise. Mixing the kefir with grated cucumber (drained of excess water) with a seasoning of dry-roasted cumin and red chili powder and garnishing with torn coriander leaves gives this simple yogurt side dish a decadent royal touch.

Fourteen years later, I am in my house in America's Finest City. I've called San Diego America's Finest City for decades—it started as a joke with my now ex—especially funny to us because it didn't make sense. Many things in America still don't make sense or seem logical to me. What makes a city America's finest? What would a "finer" city be? It reminds me still this isn't home, and yet it is. Didi's on the East Coast. We are voices on each other's phones in this land, still close, still far apart.

After Baba, Ma's now gone too, though my friends say they feel her presence when I invite them over to feed them my version of Ma's recipes. None of my friends had met her when she was alive, but most of them feel her next to me in my kitchen. They couldn't have known that Ma was a quiet presence. Or that when she spoke, she was funny, snarky. That she had a dirty sense of humor. But they feel her calm quietness in my home. In my food.

For me, Ma is a happy constant. Her shuffle, her soft call to alert me to lower the flame on the cauliflower curry. Sometimes I hear her voice when

I'm waking in the early morning—she used to be my human alarm clock. She still is.

Each time I cook fish, as I drop the onion slices in the hot oil and then the turmeric-coated fish slices after, I tell Baba, "I am now that foreigner oceans away that you used to sing about. And you still recognize me, oceans away—I am not a stranger to the lands you sang about. I am still here. And you. And you."

Melted ghee

....

CHAPTER 3

Feeding the Future Ex-in-Laws
(Mr. and Mrs. Mohgan's Able Assistant)

It isn't that Mrs. Mohgan is ill-tempered. She just doesn't have time to be social. Even though it's Mr. Mohgan's prata that everyone lines up for, for the past three decades she's the one who has managed the orders, money, and assembly line. This is Singapore, so it's hot and therefore, humid. There isn't much to say about that, except that the Mohgans have been prata sellers for as long as anyone can remember. While in India, pratas are called parathas (with the *th* pronounced not as in "thin," but with an aspirated hard inflection), in Singapore, as in many South Asian countries outside of India, the word has morphed, just as the recipe has been adapted to suit the local palate. In Singapore, a combination of Malay, Chinese, Indonesian, and Indian influence has given rise to the word and the inherently Singaporean fast food, the prata.

In fact, Mr. Mohgan was twelve when he began helping his mother at her prata stall, so it seemed natural for him to start his own when he grew up.

Mrs. Mohgan has no time for niceties. She takes the order, writes it down, rings it up, and places it. She doesn't smile. Everyone on Instagram comments on her dourness and lack of humor.[1] As if "smile more, lady" will make her do so. She is driven, hardworking, and tired. It shows in everything she does as co-owner of their coffee shop (prata kopitiam in Malay). While Malays and Indonesians may say it's a coffee stall, it's not.

It's strictly a prata stall for the Mohgans, all the time, and the world's very best, mind you.

Mrs. Mohgan takes the order in a beaten-up exercise book and informs you (sometimes) of the wait time and the order number. It usually takes half an hour on weekends for an order to be ready, somewhat less during weekdays. Then she yells out your number. The stall is small, the hot plate unwieldy with uneven heating. And the Mohgans only have one assistant, Mohammad Jihath. It's Singapore, it's hot, and therefore Mrs. Mohgan, as noted earlier, has no time for niceties, and sometimes her informing you of your order status is one nicety you'll have to do without.

In 2006 Mr. Mohgan called his store on Crane Road Mr Mohgan's Super Crispy Roti Prata. Twelve years later, he moved this coffee shop on the same road to another location and changed the name to Mr and Mrs Mohgan Super Crispy Roti Prata.[2] (The British style, with no period after the Mr or the Mrs, made it seem as if the punctuation would be too much of a stop for the indefatigable Mohgans.) Mr. Mohgan has made sure to put his wife's name on the prata stall sign. As a Singaporean whose family moved from the Indian subcontinent a few generations ago, Somasundaram Mohgan has broken the mold, taking the term "ardhangini," or life partner, literally, calling his wife his business partner.

. . . .

Maryland, 1997. I am in graduate school, finishing my PhD, almost ready to apply for postdoctoral fellowships in molecular biology. But I hesitate because, as a graduate student, my aim is to get a fellowship and a post-doctoral position in a university along with the required visa papers to stay in America legally. I do not have the luxury of choosing a university or a particular geographical location. What is important is that the fellowship enables me to get on what's called an OPT (Optional Practical Training) program for F-1 student visa holders.[3] The training period is one year. During that year, the aim for all such immigrant postgraduate students is to excel in their role in a new lab with a new professor, who is the principal investigator, holds all the grant money, and makes decisions on fellowship financing, the students' visas and therefore their lives in America, because once OPT is over, the principal investigator and the research university will decide whether or not to sponsor the postdoctoral immigrant student for an Hı professional visa. If not, then they have to return to their home country. That's why there's no option to reject an offer or negotiate better pay. As a postdoctoral fellow, one feels only gratitude for being able to continue to research and appreciation for a few extra dollars in the pay-check, followed by the next visa before the green card application. Choosing which part of America to do this work isn't an option, for me or for any immigrant in my situation. What this also means is that my marriage plans with my now ex are complicated. If I don't know which university I am headed to, how can I plan to marry? And if I do marry, how do I handle the geographical logistics with uncertainty of this magnitude?

My now ex's parents are visiting him for the first time. According to custom, which I wasn't brought up to follow but know is important to him, I realize that they will determine when we can get married. But they haven't met me yet. At the time of their 1997 visit, I am looking for a postdoctoral position with a paid fellowship. I have to choose which university to apply to. Only then can I figure out when I'll get married. I feel my life is now inexorably linked with his.

In 1997, I had been with my now ex for nearly two years, and that investment of time, love, body, and mind was sufficient for me to link my life to his. For a Bengali brought up on Bollywood movies, for a science girl raised on hope and romance in Mills & Boon books read surreptitiously during sleep-inducing Hindi literature classes, for an ambitious go-getter whose culture told her falling in love with another from her home country meant this was her forever—for that person, for me in 1997, my now ex was forever. Everything I did was to get to the stage where I would be married to him, because why does one fall in love so headlong if not for that?

. . . .

I meet him in fall 1995—I meet him and his roommates, who lived upstairs from my apartment in a predominantly Indian apartment complex, filled with graduate students, their spouses, children, and free babysitters—their parents.

When we are introduced, my now ex wears a thick red-and-gray T-shirt and faded sweatpants, as if he doesn't care how he looks. I am in my trendy, paint-splashed jeans. I think I look very American. He shakes my hand formally, his eyes darkly amused. I love him already and I don't even know him.

"Call me Sunday with a J," he says, grinning at his clever joke. It's how he asks Americans to pronounce his name. His name is a simple one, and everyone who's watched *The Simpsons* knows how to pronounce it. Even then, he says call me Sunday with a J. His roommates and I laugh at his very American wit. He is handsome, after all. And when he sings Mohammad Rafi's songs, all of us are mesmerized.

My now ex is the only one among us with a job, degree, and a second-hand Toyota. He is South Indian, tall, witty, and went to a regional engineering college in the desert. More important, he can speak Hindi. He's almost as North Indian as I am. Which is to say, we both like Punjabi food, Hindi music, and can speak Hindi fluently. It's important to me, because it seems to me most South Indians speak Tamil and struggle with any other language, even tinging their English with rolling *r*'s and hard *t*'s for no reason. Then, too, I know South Indians usually don't get my jokes, and many chant their religious mantras very seriously—whether it's after they wake up, when they get their exam results, before an interview, any time, all the time. That is my blanket generalization about all South Indians when I meet my now ex. But not my now ex. He is smooth, in fact, his English spotless, his Hindi fluent, and his sense of humor is spectacular. When I meet him the first time that evening, he raises his eyebrows in a silent, informal "hi" and then walks across the room to shake my hand, as if we are cage fighters. Only we are not. I too stick my hand out as if I am already a professional career woman, which I am not.

Later, he tells me I am trying too hard to be American. Using curse words, speaking fluent English, wearing figure-hugging jeans, listening to Pink Floyd or the Dave Matthews Band or Santana does not make you American, he says.

I don't wear those jeans again.

This is what I feel about love, about lust, about passion. If you don't let it envelop you, if you don't let it soak into you, why even try. I give myself to this completely. I don't know this new me. But I like how he makes me feel. My life is inexorably linked to his.

I want him in my life. I want to be his life.

....

When we connect, it's over food. South Indian food, like rasam, sambar, koottu—dishes I've only eaten at restaurants. I teach him about Bengali fish, about sweets, about our music. But we always get back to South Indian food. His food.

"Madhu," he says impatiently the first time I attempt to make rasam, "the tartness from the tamarind and tomato has to be balanced." What he means is that if you add too much tamarind, the tartaric acid in tamarind may take over the mild flavor from the citric acid in tomatoes in the gravy. He adds, "If you don't grow up with this, you'll never be able to make it right."

I don't argue with him. After all, I didn't grow up drinking or making rasam. From that day on, he makes the rasam.

....

Mr. Mohgan makes the prata by hand—three kinds: plain, mushroom, or egg. Each prata comes with a sauce: fish curry, dal, or sambal. Spicy, fiery red-hot curry is exactly what's needed in Singapore's hot and humid weather to dunk the crispy fried dough in as a starter breakfast or brunch food. For years Mr. Mohgan's stall on Crane Road had lines snaking all around the store and beyond. Then, in August 2018, he up and leaves. He's gone, but the prata kopitiam stall is still there, doing business.

No one notices, especially the customers, because his assistant, twenty-eight-year-old Mohammad Jihath still tosses the artisanal pratas in the current location—run now by a quiet thirty-one-year-old mother and businesswoman, Jamaldeen Yosliya. She tells curious food bloggers and Instagrammers that Mr. Mohgan retired and gave her the stall along with the assistant for S$15,000. She changes the name to Famous Crispy Prata Indian Muslim Food. Jihath knows how to flip pratas, and Yosliya gets the customers, who show up mistakenly thinking the shop is Mr. Mohgan's. The only way to keep them is to continue to make the pratas as good as Mr. Mohgan's. All the customers—regulars—show up and appreciate the food. Great breakfast combo, the sambals still as flavorful and spicy, the pratas still as crispy.

....

Ma cannot make Tamilian dishes—we don't know what to do with a combination of asafetida, curry leaves, tamarind, and mustard seeds. We also don't know what to do with families who are vegetarian by religion and choice. In my home, a vegetarian meal is tolerated with annoyance and worry—are they too poor to get fish? Did someone die and so they had to mourn them by eliminating fish and meat from their daily meals? Were they all widows, because they are vegetarian or supposed to be, according to Bengali Hindu culture? But then, here I am, in love with this tall, handsome man, with a wicked sense of humor, a raspy voice meant for singers, a man brought up among them and as vegetarian as ever.

Baba said, "A vegetarian is a cow that mistakenly was born a human," which wouldn't go over well with my now ex's family, I am sure.

My now ex is and was then, a man of contradictions. When I meet him, he's a lapsed vegetarian. He eats chicken as much as I do. He's not a "practicing Brahmin," as we say. He still wears his poonal, his sacred thread, in 1997, announcing to the world his high-caste Brahmin status. He will abandon that poonal in a couple of years, but back then he is connected to his traditional religious roots, even though he doesn't bring attention to it the way I've seen other South Indian Brahmin men do. Regardless, he's Brahmin, a higher caste, still holding on to the religious connection— the "holy" thread that connects him to his caste, god, and righteousness. We don't discuss this, but likely when he was a teenager, there was a religious ceremony in which his parents sat down with the priest, prayed to their gods, draping him with the poonal for the first time, chanting the

Gayatri mantra, the secret Sanskrit code that only Brahmin men traditionally chanted to the gods[4]—and he promised all the holy deities never to take the poonal off, never to eat meat, never to swear or curse, and to be kind and pray righteously as a good upper-caste Brahmin would.

When I meet him, we bond by competing over who can use more swear words in our sentences. Even though he tells me not to swear in front of others, when we are alone we can play the who-swears-more-and-better game like children. I win, mostly, because I am competitive like that. He likes it when we have these imaginary battles—one of us has to win. It's our joke, it's our attraction, we are Type A and we know it.

We are together all the time. I cook, he helps. He cooks, I help. We are together, and it's electric, the way we are. If this were a Hindi movie, we are in this stage of the movie and love story: the leading lady and man have sung their songs in foreign locales, the lady is wrapped gracefully in fluttering saris, her hair flowing, the man sweeps his hands in the air with loud proclamations of love. After that, the next step is marriage. Hindi movies inform me on how my life should be. Even though I am in Maryland for graduate school, my life is governed by Bollywood—and how!

I've already told Ma and Baba, who are waiting to meet him. They remain in India but expect him to visit, us to visit. We Ghoshes are still traditional, even though we are progressive. But that visit may be in a few months, a year. Not yet. His parents, however, are coming to see him next month—it will be their first time in this country. I am giddy because they will meet me. The woman their son chose. The woman their son loves. The feminist Bengali. The scientist Bengali. They will meet me. They will meet me. That's the next step.

I am a creature of habit. I know this has to end in marriage—and why should it not? I have invested my youth, my heart, and being in this. I have shown him what it means to be mine, and for me to be his. If you follow logic, first comes love and then comes marriage.

It's 1997. I am meeting his parents for the first time in my life.

. . . .

Jihath massages the dough with oil, layering it in with each pat of his expert hands on the soft, kneaded flour. He adds more vegetable shortening to make each dough ball squishy. He kneads the dough for about a thousand portions each day with Ikan Terbung low-protein wheat flour and a secret combination of sugar, salt, eggs, margarine, and shortening along with the ubiquitous clarified butter.

He's young, brash, and obviously the brains of the operation behind the Muslim prata stall. Yosliya depends on him for all the recipes—not just the prata but also the curries. All she has brought here is a younger staff and her hopes for a younger, hip Singaporean clientele.

Then, two months later, the crowd thins. Very few queue up for the Famous Crispy Prata Indian Muslim Food. The regulars all but disappear. What's going on, Yosliya wonders. Was the quality not as good? Is this Ramadan? Did someone spread rumors? Did Jihath change the recipes?

. . . .

The parents visit his studio apartment. They say, "Oh ho, it's too small. How will we stay here?"

They head back to his sister's, seventy miles away—she lives in a suburban small town in Pennsylvania in a two-story, four-bedroom house with stained wall-to-wall carpeting, a barfing newborn son, an older daughter from a previous marriage, and two very beautiful but neglected Rottweilers. Camp Hill, a suburb of Harrisburg is a village with a Main Street, a BJ's, a Walmart, and hardly any Indians.

To correct this issue of his parents staying at his sister's instead of his place, my now ex decides to move to a one-bedroom apartment, seven miles from my apartment. I help him move. I carry his heavy futon mattress. We use my secondhand hatchback to move his things from the studio to the apartment because my car fits more boxes and he doesn't want to spoil his new Accord, an upgrade from the Toyota. We move things till 11 p.m. because his parents will come over from his sister's by midafternoon the next day.

"Madhu, you don't have to be here," he tells me, "I'll call you when they're here."

"Okay," I say.

I acquiesce to what he wants me to do, like a submissive girlfriend who does what she's told. I don't question what I have turned into. I like how he makes me feel.

. . . .

Five hundred and fifty yards, or nearly six football fields away from the Famous Crispy Prata Indian Muslim Foodstall, Mr. Mohgan opens his stall as "Mr and Mrs Mohgan's Prata Stall" eight weeks after he "retires." The same pratas—plain, mushroom, egg. The same sauces—fish, sambal, and dal. This stall is the real deal, only a seven-minute walk from its original spot.

Yosliya finds out from one of the customers who was her regular for eight weeks and then abandoned her stall to return to Mr. Mohgan. She follows the snaking lines and gets ahold of Mr. Mohgan.

Likely, Yosliya asks Mr. Mohgan, "Hey, I gave you S$15,000 for your stall, your customers, and took over the rent. Why are you now my competition? What's going on?"

Likely, Mr. Mohgan says, "I didn't say I was going to retire forever!"

To which Yosliya replies, "Well, that must be some short retirement for sure, give me my money back."

Instagram foodies inform us that she gets most of her money back, now that the customers are a trickling percentage of the opening numbers.[5] She's fine with that, because she knows Jihath knows the recipes. There is room for more than one crispy prata stall in Singapore.

. . . .

Every evening when I return from the lab, I call my now ex. He is busy with his parents. He takes them to the Washington monuments in the evenings, the temple over weekends, to American restaurants where they eat pizza the way they would yogurt rice at home. They spend their time arranging, rearranging his furniture and alphabetizing his CD collection. They use his futon mattress as their bed. They don't complain. He sleeps in a sleeping bag in the front room. They don't mind that despite his being a consultant in a global IT firm, he still lives like he's a graduate student. Once the parents arrive, he doesn't invite me over anymore. Not that they don't know who I am; they do. But the official introduction is still pending. I don't want to disturb South Indian sentiments. After all, I am going to marry their son. I'll wait, I say to anyone who asks me—friends, Didi, Ma—I'll wait, I say. I'll wait, I think.

"What did you cook for dinner," I ask him one evening when I call him after I return to my apartment from the lab.

"Oh, I don't cook anymore. Ma's the best cook in the world. She's making things that I've been dreaming of since I moved here!" he says. In the background, I hear his mother's faintly masculine voice laugh with pride—eavesdropping on her son's conversation is natural to her, it appears.

I feel a very unfamiliar pang of jealousy when I hear that. But I cook very well, I want to whine. I cook extremely well, I want to yell. You always said I am an excellent cook, especially chicken tikka masala. I want to say all that, but I don't.

"That's nice," I say politely.

Another week goes by. I wait next to the phone every evening after my day in the lab. My roommate, Aarti, a microbiology graduate student, watches me, shaking her head in disapproval. "Madhushree, he will invite you when he's ready. Don't do this to yourself."

I smile back at her. "Oh, no, I'm not doing anything. It's okay. I'm sure he'll get his parents to meet me soon."

Her eyes are so sad when she looks at me that I have to look away. I don't question what I have turned into.

. . . .

Jihath's coin pratas—sugar-filled pratas twisted into Cinnabon-like rolls—are sweet, sugary, and crispy with shortening and butter. The sauces for fish, sambal, and dal are similar to Mr. Mohgan's, but certainly much hotter. Jihath feels that's what makes customers come back for more. Lately, however, they have been more watery and inconsistent.

In his new digs, Mr. Mohgan has tables, twice as many seats as in his previous joint, a whirring ceiling fan, and many more parking spots than earlier. Location, location, location indeed. Mrs. Mohgan continues to be curmudgeonly, taking orders with the surliest expression she can muster. She doesn't have to call the order readiness out—the blinking sign tells the customer to get their prata pronto. People wait maybe half the amount of time they had to earlier. It's certainly been a win-win situation for Mr. and Mrs. Mohgan. The Instagrammers tell Mr. Mohgan that Jihath is serving a thousand pratas every day.

He laughs dismissively, "If I'm alone in the store, I only do five hundred. Anyone who does twice as much is Superman!"

Everyone wonders if he's afraid of the competition from his Muslim assistant just a few doors away. "No," he says, "just knowing the proportions doesn't mean you can make a good crispy prata. Each of my assistants knows only one part of the recipe. I'm the only one who has all the knowledge. I know everything."

He doesn't use shortening, ghee is his go-to, and every ball of dough is hand-stretched and massaged by him. That's his secret and he doesn't hide it. He now has a new hot plate and three assistants. Mr. Mohgan is certainly the king of crispy prata, now back from retirement.

. . . .

One month after his parents have been with him, I put my foot down.

"Shall I come over, or will you bring them to my place?" I don't give him a chance to refuse.

"We can always meet you later, Madhu," he starts.

"No. I'm making dinner. Aarti will be there too. They can meet her and me. She's South Indian. They can have conversations with her if they feel out of place with a Bengali."

He sighs, "Why is it always this with you? Who said anything about you being a Bengali?"

The problem is that we have said nothing about nothing. I assume we will get married. I assume he knows. I assume his parents know. I assume they know how important it is to me. It is. I wonder if it's more important than my PhD.

"Tomorrow. 7 p.m. Bring them, please. Dinner will be ready."

That evening, I make dinner. Aarti—who can't cook like I can—vacuums the small apartment, cleans the bathroom, then sets the table. I make masoor dal with cumin, nigella seeds, ginger, and turmeric. I make begun bhaja, frying the eggplant in mustard oil just like Ma taught me. I add sugar at the end to caramelize the eggplant slices before serving. Then I make cauliflower curry with frozen peas and a roasted cumin-and-coriander seasoning. I finish that with a raita—cucumber and tomatoes in thick yogurt seasoned with Kashmiri mirch and cumin. After that, I make ghee from unsalted butter, slowly stirring the whey away from the oils to make a thick dark brown liquid. The apartment fills with its fragrant smell. The sweet yogurt with soft jaggery notes is setting in the fridge. We are ready.

．．．．．．．．．．．．．．．

Jihath handles the dough like an artiste—his movements are delicate and deliberate, like a ballet dancer. He doesn't waver even when crowds peak. By contrast, Mr. Mohgan moves fast and flips the pratas quickly. He's good, especially on weekdays, and his pratas are crispy when the wait is short. On long wait times, the chewiness of the pratas may be suspect, though dousing them in the sauces makes up for the quality control issues. The fish and mutton curries are thick, rich, and luxurious, and as always, consistently and predictably good. Mr. Mohgan's sambal is made with anchovies, dried chili, belacan (shrimp paste), garlic, and onions, making this more Malaysian than Singaporean. All this leads to an otherworldly culinary experience. And it's also S$0.50 more expensive than Jihath's, but worth it.

．．．．．．．．．．．．．．．

The family that I want to belong to shows up promptly at 7 p.m. Later, my now ex and his mother tell me that it's not them but his father who's the punctual one. His father, a tall man in his sixties with my now ex's nose smiles politely and offers me a formal handshake. He wears a skull cap and a thick sweater, even though it's not that cold in Maryland yet.

His mother, small, with thick eyebrows, and with foundation on her face that's ten shades lighter than her skin tone, making her look ashy, awkwardly clings to my now ex's arm and says, "Hi, Madhu," like a child.

Later I find out that everyone says she, Annie, is like a child. Annie, a name given to her in the '60s when she was newly married to my now ex's father and lived in England for four years. Annie is like a child. Everyone says she's a great cook, but she's the youngest in her family, and a child. That description sticks. I don't know what it means. Does it mean she's childlike, innocent? Or childish like a grown woman acting petulantly? I don't know, but as long as I knew her, she was Annie, who is "such a child," such a naïve and innocent person that everybody forgave her behavior without much protest.

Twenty years ago, she must have been in her late fifties, early sixties. She wasn't a child. But in 1997, I know that this is my mother-in-law-to-be, so I smile back at her and say, "Welcome."

They admire our sparse furniture, the secondhand bookshelf tilting to the right from the weight of all the biochemistry books. Aarti's television and overstuffed couch sit in the living room adjacent to the dining area—the only two things in the graduate students' apartment that are relatively new. The dining table has my mother's blue tablecloth, hiding the scratches from our carrying it upstairs from near the dumpster where another graduate student left it.

"Good house, Madhu," his father says, even though I know it's not.

Next to him, I see my now ex exhale. That's when I realize, it is his father who will make all the decisions. It is his father we all try to get on our side.

"Let's eat, the food will get cold," I say, clearing my throat, pretending to be in charge.

Aarti puts the rice bowl in the center. I bring the cauliflower over. The parents head one by one to the tiny bathroom to wash their hands—they will obviously eat with their hands. While I have changed my eating habits in the years since I moved from India. Though I can go back to C. R. Park and eat Ma's food with my fingers with the same ease I always have, I eat with a fork in America now.

We ask if they want wine. His father doesn't drink, but my now ex goads him to. He acquiesces, but it really wasn't much of a protest to begin with. We open a bottle—I think it's merlot, but we aren't aficionados. Who knows what we open? I bring out my Pier 1 champagne flutes because that's all we have in terms of wine glasses. No one cares. We toast, and his mother wipes the wine stain from her lips with the pallu of her sari when she thinks no one is looking.

I serve the ghee I made that evening to his father first. A dollop on the steaming white rice. I push the salt closer so he can mix the starchy rice with the fragrant clarified knuckle-deep in the rice-and-ghee mix on his plate.

"Thank you," I grin.

The apartment is filled with lip-smacking and chewing sounds. Ma always said those sounds are uncouth, low class. You can be a Brahmin and still be low class, I think. Then I shake myself out of that judgmental attitude—I am after all, marrying into this family. They're old, that's why they eat with their mouths open. I will make this work.

We talk a lot and laugh a lot. They tell me they think Bengalis sing Rabindra sangeet and eat roshogolla every day. They tell me how different we are from them. They ask me if I believe in god.

I say, "No, I grew up in a family where this wasn't a priority. Education was—is."

My now ex's father nods, "But we do. Believe in god, you know?"

"Sure," I say. "I won't stop you and you shouldn't stop me. Hisaab baraabar."

Yes, he nods. Fair is fair, we settled accounts. I don't need to put you down, and you don't need to challenge me either.

"The ghee, Madhu," he says again, "this is excellent. How did you make it?"

"Oh, it's easy, unsalted butter. You need the best organic butter and keep it on low simmer. Simple, but the whey has to separate from the clarified butter."

"Is it that simple, Madhu?" he asks.

I nod, happy to share the information, "It is, but it's also a science experiment. You have to watch or else you can burn it. Then it'll taste bitter with burnt fatty solids from the cream. You can't undercook it or it'll have that faint raw milk smell. It's a fine balance."

Aarti announces, before I can stop her, "Madhushree is a very good cook, Uncle."

He nods appreciatively. My now ex watches him closely.

Then my now ex says, "But Mom makes good ghee too, na, Ma?"

I hadn't noticed his mother's reaction till then. She sits with her fingers coated with masoor dal and rice, a petulant mouth, with an expression holding the beginnings of a tantrum.

She looks up at her husband to her left, across from me, and says, "Enna, isn't my ghee good?"

"Aw, Annie," her husband says, as if on autopilot, a reassurance and a soft teasing pattern that married couples often fall into, "Are you jealous now that I praised Madhu?"

No, she shakes her head and says, "My ghee is good."

My now ex reaches across the table, his left hand outstretched to his mother, "Your ghee is the best, Ma," he says decisively.

I head to the kitchen to bring out the jaggery-sweetened mishti doi. Aarti follows me and places her empty plate in the sink.

. . . .

When Mr. Mohgan is asked about his expansion plans, he says he will open five more kopitiams. His assistants will manage, and he will travel from one stall to the next to ensure quality control. Even after he sold his original spot, the regulars and the foodies still come to him.

Instagrammers ask Jihath what his future plans are. In 2018, Jihath is enterprising and full of ideas. He says, surreptitiously watching out for his employer, "I'll open my own kopitiam soon."

Online, the Instagrammers instantly tattle. Yosliya, when she hears about it, says in a soft but determined voice, "Oh, well, I'll get another assistant. The stall will continue. There can always be another prata place, and mine is good."

It's not that Mr. Mohgan won. Or Yosliya lost. It's just a promise broken and another betrayal and yet another expectation dashed. It's also the establishment of a known cook over an upstart who has employed another upstart. It isn't personal. It's just survival in a commoditized prata world in Singapore.

We haven't heard yet about Jihath's stall opening. But it is only a matter of time.

It's the pandemic now, so one must wait. It will happen.

. . . .

The next week, Annie invites me to my now ex's apartment. I wear a red sari and bring her carnations because I love carnations and I want to take my now ex's mother flowers that I love and hope that she will too. I try to be as Indian as I can be—no, *more* South Indian is what I try to be.

Annie's so happy to see the red flowers that she hugs me, reaching up to hold me awkwardly around my waist. My now ex doesn't have fancy cookware or matching plates. Annie cooks in battered steel pots and pans that he had brought from Madras—now Chennai—five years ago on his first-ever international flight out of India to Maryland. We sit at the IKEA table that I helped him assemble before his parents arrived from Harrisburg.

Annie ladles fragrant papaya and pumpkin koottu on my plate, then rasam and bean curry with coconut. I lick my fingers, overtly showing appreciation.

She pushes the steel katori with ghee in it. "Try it, try it, Madhu," she insists. Her eyes are anxious. I cannot say no.

The ghee isn't as brown as mine and has a faint milky smell. It's not the ghee I'm used to, but I have been taught by my parents to be polite.

"It's lovely, Annie," I lie.

Gleefully turning to her husband, she exclaims, "See? My ghee is better, even Madhu says so."

He smiles at her. She won, his eyes say. She won, my now ex's exhale says.

Beside him, my now ex says casually, "I always said Ma's an excellent cook."

There are times when one knows one has to back away. There are times when the gut says, this isn't you, this isn't for you. And one does it anyway. There are times when one knows this is the long haul, and the long haul doesn't need such histrionics. And yet. And yet. There's Bollywood. There's type A. There's a will to succeed. Then there's a father's daughter who wants to show him she's made an excellent choice. Even when she's unsure. This is that time. I do not back away.

"Your mother is an excellent cook," I say convincingly.

. . . .

Mr. Mohgan, who earlier had said he wouldn't expand, he wouldn't make more than five hundred pratas per day, he wouldn't use machinery to make the pratas as they need his touch—not anybody else's, but his touch—now says he may open a few stalls. Sometimes, even when the prata isn't as crispy, it is still famous. And if it's famous and helps Somasundaram Mohgan sell more, enough to put his two daughters through college, why not? After all, the world knows about Mr and Mrs Mohgan's Crispy Prata stall in the Joo Chiat and Dunman Road junction at Tin Yeung restaurant.

The Muslim stall is just an offshoot. The owner is just a young mother, trying to be a businesswoman. The cook is a young man who learnt from Mr. Mohgan and didn't learn fully. Sometimes age, experience, and drive beats enterprising youngsters.

Lamb curry

....

CHAPTER 4

In Search of Goat Curry
(Bunny Chow)

E very weekend in the late seventies and all of the eighties in Chittaranjan Park, Baba and I head to the weekend market on a chicken
and goat meat expedition. Saturday lunch and dinner are chicken.
Sunday lunch is goat curry and dinner is keema, or minced goat curry,
with peas. As Bengalis, we eat fish daily, and meat is a weekend affair. The
one thing the Ghosh family is known for is routine—we are creatures
of habit, and we like it that way. Even if the world turned upside down,
our lives would revolve around food, the next meal, and what Baba and I
brought from Market No. 1 for Ma to make for us.

....

I don't remember now who used to sell the Saturday chicken at the market.
Perhaps it's because they were Hindus. Otherwise, we would have certainly
talked about it. Only if someone was from a different region or religion
was it a matter of discussion—to understand why they were a bit different
from us and why it was okay for them to be since they were from a different culture or believed in a different god. It wasn't a quaint "we lived in
harmony" observation. Lines of religion, state, and culture were viciously
drawn by local rulers or Western colonizers and were adhered to by nationalist leaders who had their own selfish political motivations to do so.

Once drawn, religion reinforced the divisions. There were caste lines drawn for centuries to stop a higher caste man from marrying a lower caste woman that are still maintained today. There were all-Muslim or all-Hindu villages, separated through trade—leather goods craftspeople were mainly Muslim, certain textile and sari weavers were Hindu, each marrying and staying within their region, religion, and trade. Why, even C. R. Park and Kalkaji, two South Delhi neighborhoods, were distinctly different—one, cultured, middle-class Bengali refugees working in bureaucratic jobs in banks and the government; the other, brash, hardworking, finance-focused Sikhs and Punjabis starting their own gurudwaras and cycle repair or water pump shops.

Middle- and upper-middle-class families like ours remained traditional but not necessarily religious. Caste lines were acknowledged but not adhered to. What remained then was that we obeyed what our parents and their parents passed down through the generations. An unsaid rule, but a rule nonetheless, which was to stay within those invisible boundaries. It was as always, taken as the order in life, to keep order for life. And rules weren't meant to be broken.

....

The chicken shop in Market No. 1 is in the middle of the asbestos- or tin-roofed open-air market. Surrounded by wire cages filled with white-feathered chickens, the shop owner sits inside with a rusted biscuit tin to hold his cash. Every Saturday morning, Baba and I first stop at the chicken store.

Baba says, "Konta?"

Perfunctorily, I point at one bird at random—there is no logic to my choice—and get a skinned, quartered chicken in a plastic bag for Baba to carry. I say that with confidence because, to date, I don't remember ever being horrified that a chicken met its death because I pointed at her.

These days, when I see pristine chicken pieces separated into thighs and breasts—almost like viewing preferences on readily available porn sites in America—glistening in sealed cling-wrapped boxes at the grocery store, I wonder whether children growing up here will ever know that an animal died for them to get the nourishment they need to become good people?

At least, that's what Baba drilled into me every Saturday, "Without fish and chicken, a Bengali isn't a Bengali. Without meat, you cannot do the things you were brought into this world to do."

In the seventies, such proclamations were taken as gospel. We ate chicken on Saturdays and goat meat on Sundays. We grew up to do the things we were meant to do—what they were, wasn't of consequence. What only mattered was that Baba made sure that the best food he could afford graced his household.

. . . .

South African naturalized American, Caren Mair, who moved to San Diego by way of London, proudly holds on to her strong Durban accent tinged with a British lilt. She remembers bunny chow with the same fondness with which I salivate over the thought of spicy aloo samosas from Lucknow—food I'd eaten almost four decades ago.

"We only got the lamb bunny chows when we were kids," she says, "and we never wondered why they were called bunny even though there was lamb in the bread. We loved it, it was familiar like burgers are here."

"Yes, but why lamb?" I ask.

Caren shrugs, "You know as children, one never questions such things. A bunny was lamb and that was that."

Bunny, as it's referred to in Durban, where it was created, has a darker history than a wistful childhood memory.[1] According to food and culture author Ishay Govender, bunny chow was thought to have been first invented as a fusion food by Indians or the merchant-class businesspeople called baniya in Hindi, the food or chow was shortened to bunny chow, with no connection to rabbit.[2]

Indians arrived in South Africa around the 1860s as indentured labor for the Durban sugarcane fields. Later, business-class Indians settled in Durban, creating one of the largest immigrant Indian groups outside India. As often happens with fusion, most classes, cultures, and spices flattened, became one-dimensional, outside the home country. Bunny chow, however, was the exception because of the garam masala mix. The Durban spice mix used in South African Indian cuisine is uniquely South African—because of the difficulty of transporting spices from the native country, it is quite different from garam masala combinations from India.

Bunny chow evolved as a sandwich that didn't require utensils, designed primarily for the worker class, in particular for the South African sugarcane plantation laborers—blacks or "coloreds," the term still used for mixed-race South Africans, and the indentured Indians. It was to be a no-fuss sandwich that didn't require sitting down to eat, which was another way of enforcing apartheid.

. . . .

Across the next lane and closer to the end of the market abutting B Block of the neighborhood was Mukim, our Muslim butcher's shop. I did ask Didi recently if his name was indeed Mukim, because that's what we called him, but I hadn't heard of that name as a Muslim one—or otherwise. Didi had no idea either, so Mukim is who he was to us in 1978 and he remains Mukim to me now.

Mukim was always in a lungi, which Muslims wore—a cotton sarong-like cloth woven with a blue or green base with Madras plaid designs, tied at the hip with a knot tucked under his half-sleeve baniyan. The shirt was covered with meat bits and speckled blood from the animals he butchered. The specks were a cheery bright red, a gruesome reminder of the act that led to the blood spatter. But that wasn't something that made Baba or me cringe. Didi, much like Ma, didn't venture into smelly meat and fish stalls. So it was always Baba and me. Me and Baba. Baba and I—bonding as father and daughter in today's parlance—made it our mission to head to such shacks selling carcasses of animals we converted later into mouth-watering curries, which didn't bother either one of us because we were there, and we were there together.

Mukim must have been a young man, but he carried himself with a seriousness that the chicken boys didn't, so my childhood memories of

Mukim are that he was old and serious, which may or may not be true at all.

. . . .

As Ishay tells me when we discuss bunny chow, the Durban curry is an anomaly. It's primarily because South Africans and Indian immigrants to South Africa are passionate about this now national dish, and yet it is hardly understood by Indians from the mainland. The flavors are fierce, with multiple layers of spice and oil giving it a Hindu religious fiery saffron color, contained in a quarter pound hollowed-out loaf of bread. Ishay describes the taste and flavor of a bunny chow as relentlessly spicy, oily, and linear—comfort food at its best.

There are many restaurants that claim to have invented bunny chow.[3] According to local lore, Ranchod Patel, father of Manilal Patel and owner of Durban's oldest Gujarati food canteen, Patel's Vegetarian Refreshment Room, was the one who made the first vegetarian bunny chow for sale. Tripadvisor posts from satisfied visitors have claimed the bunny to be the same authentic taste for the past nine decades. Billy and Kanagee Moodley of the Victory Lounge, which opened less than a decade after Patel's and recently closed, credit Kapitan's restaurant at the Victory Lounge as the original location of the bunny chow dish.[4] The first group to invent this uniquely South African dish could simply just have been Indian households. More likely, the racial segregation laws that prohibited the sale of food at a sit-down restaurant to Blacks and coloreds made this dish a necessary and innovative invention. Restaurants skirted the law by selling the same food out the back door, conveniently making cheap white bread the food holder and transporter.

"Don't forget," Ishay cautions me, "this was meant for the Black and brown people—cheap and affordable food. There was nothing glamorous about the dish, as it were."

Still another origin theory is that since bread was a convenient way to transport the curry, bunny chow was made for blue-collar workers, likely indentured laborers or caddies for golf courses who weren't allowed a long lunch break. Bunny chow is meant to be eaten using one's fingers, as we used to back home. Just as pizza eaten with a fork and knife in America gets eye rolls, anybody eating bunny chow with cutlery is considered suspect. I grew up eating with my fingers, and I assume that bunny chow was also meant for people like me, who had no use for cutlery. When first served as takeout, bunny chow was served in newspapers, much like samosas and jalebis in India. It is only recently that the dish is served in to-go containers to reduce the spill of spicy oil and curry.

. . . .

Mukim was an expert in skinning, paring, and chopping goat in minutes with his large shiny knife and mallet. If he wasn't chopping through bones and removing fascia from the muscle, he was running his knife on the whetstone, splashing water on it from a dirty plastic bucket next to the tree stump block he used to cut the meat on. Behind him, there was always a Bollywood superstar Amitabh Bachchan movie soundtrack playing from his radio, which hung from a wooden hook on the wall behind him. Sometimes the music was about friendship and how friends would never break the promise of being there for each other[5] or about who would be king of his destiny in "Woh muqaddar ka sikandar, jaaneman kehlayega."[6] Every song played on his transistor radio echoed in his thatch-roofed stall, with movie superstars on open roads declaring love, friendship, and joy, certainly a far cry from Mukim butchering meat in sweltering heat in his tiny shop in C. R. Park.

I remember thinking he liked Kishore Kumar's voice—a legendary playback singer then and a Bengali, much to our delight—but now I realize that it was primarily music from films such as *Don, Muqaddar ka sikandar,* and *Deewar* that he preferred. Perhaps Mukim, in his lungi and baniyan with blood spatter had dreams of Bollywood, being an actor or a superhero in his little meat shop—an ambition most Indians like us nurtured growing up. Or perhaps Mukim just liked Amitabh Bachchan, the superstar of 1970s and 1980s Bollywood, the only star who has now graduated to roles that were unheard of in those days. Known then as the Angry Young Man,

Bachchan is now nearing eighty, towering still, but an old man. I wonder what Mukim listens to these days.

. . . .

It didn't matter if it was a Muslim festival or a Ramadan fast, Mukim's shop was always open for us on weekends. Every visit I made, I'd see him at his stand, on a platform of about two feet. I knew he'd be chopping the meat into keema, minced by deliberate thwacks of his shiny blade, even though, as a religious man, he himself fasted. While he and Baba didn't talk much except to discuss which part of the goat to cut, they each danced this soft dance of mutual understanding and respect for the other—Mukim knew how to butcher and Baba knew which part of the goat to take home. Mukim sometimes suggested lamb, which tasted less fatty but was still rich in flavor. I don't think Baba ever ventured into the brave new world of trying lamb.

"Double pack it, Mukim, I don't want the packet leaking." Baba reminded him each time.

"Dada," Mukim said softly, "you know I will." Each time.

We rushed to the chicken shop to pick up the very dead and very quartered chicken, then to the vegetable seller for paneer, coriander leaves, and onions before heading back to Mukim for the heavy double-bagged goat meat.

Mukim never argued with Baba about money. The only speaking he did was with how he cut and quartered the meat. That was his job, and I know now, an art.

. . . .

Back in the kitchen at home, the goat meat was always made first, since the meat is more difficult to cook. It needed tenderizing, so Ma marinated it with spices, yogurt and oil. The Bengali style is simpler than North Indian ways of making goat curry, but still needed acid, spice mixes, and whole inflammation-reducing spices to reduce the gaminess of the meat. Ma cooks the red meat with spices used in tandoori oven baking: cardamom,

IN SEARCH OF GOAT CURRY   57

ginger-and-garlic paste, cloves, and cinnamon, along with garam masala powder (a ground mix of the mostly Cs—cloves, cardamom, cinnamon, plus cumin, coriander, chili powder, black pepper, and nutmeg).

While we used to hear of mothers spending most Saturdays slow cooking the curries on gas stoves, Ma accelerated hers by using a pressure cooker instead of a tandoori oven. Still, on Saturdays, our house always smelled of ginger, garlic, and onion, while the pressure cooker whistles interrupted all conversations in my childhood.

Ma's only advice to Didi and me on cooking was "Don't spend more than twenty minutes in the kitchen—your world should be around conversations, not in front of a stove."

Her recipe certainly told us how quickly we could cook in a pressure cooker. It was simple, flavorful, and made to fit the life of a harried cook, an expert, and someone who valued the texture and taste of a meal made with love.

. . . .

After the goat curry was cooked, Ma let the meat soak up the spices overnight in the fridge—by Sunday, the curry was rich, thick with flavor, bursting with the spice of ginger and the zing of sautéed onions and garam masala.

Saturday chicken with rice: the turmeric jhol colored my fingernails yellow. Didi and I considered it a matter of pride and joy to lick our fingers for the last drop of the sauce. But Sunday goat curry lunch was what I lived for. It was heavier, needing more rice to sop up the curry, and was frankly the only thing I wanted to eat for lunch.

But there was an order in which to eat our food—start with greens, then dal, then vegetable curry, and then the goat curry—moving sequentially from a lighter, more easily digested curry to a heavier one. A Bengali meal is never a buffet where you dump spinach with paneer next to your naan and throw the chicken curry on top.

On Sundays the rules of the Ghosh household were that I didn't get to the goat curry unless I ate my vegetables. I'd eat them to get to the meat at the end of the meal. Such was the lure of goat curry.

After a decadent lunch every Sunday, Didi and I slept. The afternoon sun streamed in from the window in our room. We used to lay in bed, limbs at impossible awkward angles, a leg touching another in a careless abandon only children have at a very certain time of their childhood.

. . . .

Then, just like that, childhood was done.

I move to America. I don't know how to cook anything Ma used to make because I spent my childhood eating and studying—the two things Ma and Baba wanted me to do. Those are the rules too. Study and eat—you listen to your parents. You study. You eat. You aren't prepared for anything else. Especially not moving to a new country, a different continent, alone, for the first time in your life. You aren't prepared.

. . . .

1993, I am in Long Island, New York. I have a three-speed bike, abandoned behind our lab last summer, that I make my own. I ride it to a large supermarket in the small village where I've been since I landed in America. The market is open 24/7. It has chicken in packages; jumbo-sized fruit, tomatoes, and root vegetables are available year round as tasteless objects that masquerade as food. It is 1993. Organic food is still unknown in Long Island. But this is America. It is where I wanted to be since I was a child. There is no goat curry, no goat meat, no Sunday that feels like Sunday. I have to adjust. This is being an adult. This is homesickness.

. . . .

It is almost two decades after I arrived when I finally try to make goat curry in America. It is daunting—and frankly, America is a goat meat desert. What am I to add? What am I to marinate it with? The meat looks too dark. It's too dense. What spices? How many cloves? Will yogurt do?

Or kefir? It was too scary to even attempt for the first few years. It was only after moving to San Diego, home to many organic farms and sustainably farmed animals, fruits, and vegetables, that I venture out looking to build a relationship with the neighborhood butcher and perhaps get to know the farmer.

The neighborhood grocery store where I live is expensive, meant for privileged white people, stocked with organic, fresh, sustainable foods from local farms. I live in abundance and I am aware of it, yet there are no live animals for sale in an open-air market. The disconnect is obvious. I have lived in this country longer than I have in India, so the disconnect really shouldn't be there, but it is. I notice the absence of things. There aren't blood spatters on counters or on butchers' aprons, and the knives are clean, sanitized, gleaming. In fact, large animals are already quartered into manageable sizes, resembling nothing but fat and muscle, sitting cleanly on sterile-looking deli shelves, next to an electric automated saw that would make smaller pieces of that nondescript piece of muscle and fat, without any significant human effort.

I don't know if Mukim is still in Market No. 1 in C. R. Park. When I did visit a few years ago, after my parents were long gone, it wasn't to stay in the house that Baba built but at a school friend's place in a glitzy suburb far away from C. R. Park. My visit to the house I used to call home is rushed, hurried, scattered, and short. I go past the market and am stunned by how much it has changed. It now has double-storied brick buildings with stalls of fast foods, takeout, and sundries shops. The construction appears to have been rapid, haphazard, with no regard for safety or building codes. Some of the buildings appear crooked, as if the quickly constructed foundation has led to them mimicking the Leaning Tower of Pisa, but certainly not in an aesthetically pleasing way.

Only a few of the older mishti shops remain, selling the sticky sweet roshogolla, ledikini, milk cake, and mishti doi. I step into Kamala Sweets, the sweet shop that was a favorite growing up. They package the sweets in smart plasticware and give out small wooden spoons to eat them with, unlike the newspaper or flimsy cardboard boxes they packed them in when I was a child. The market is brightly lit, with electric wires still hanging dangerously low from every imaginable corner.

The vegetable market is sanitized along with the meat shops. Everything is refrigerated, and everything is packaged with an excess of plastic wrap. I don't really go looking for Mukim or his goat meat shop the last time I visit. There is no reason to, is what I think. I cannot picture him in this new, modernized market.

In the San Diego local organic market, there are signs of abundant sanitation efforts near the meat counter. The polite butcher from Mexico with a laminated name tag on his apron always has a smile on his face, his hands carefully protected in nitrile gloves. No electric wires hang dangerously close to the streets, nor does the air smell of fried samosas and chicken hakka noodles. But this is all I have, and this is now home.

The butcher looks at me, still with a polite smile, waiting as I make my choice. There isn't goat meat here. The closest to it is organic lamb from a farm close to the border. Baba would have never bought it—it doesn't compare to goat. I settle for lamb.

. . . .

The flavor profile in all bunny chow creations has remained the same. Perhaps the oil has been reduced or ghee is not used, but the spices—cumin, coriander, mace, nutmeg—are from South Africa and consistent. According to Spice Emporium, managed by Chandrika Harie in Durban, Indians couldn't go back to their home country as easily as they can now.[7] As a way of still keeping that connection, the spices were grown in African soil, with seeds pilfered and stored in shirt pockets and knots in saris, traveling across oceans to get to Durban. The spice mixes used in the chow were likely influenced by multiple cultures—the generic label "Indian" may have included Sri Lankan, South Indian, Gujarati, and North Indian people, all adding their flavor preferences to the bunny chow to make it what it is now. This mix created a dish that reminded immigrants from South

Asia of a land they'd long left, flavored by the land where they arrived and made their own.

·············

The one rule of Ma's that I've diligently stood by is the twenty-minute one. I try to cook like her and fail usually, but I certainly keep my cooking down to as short a time as possible. Most discerning guests who come to my home feel my ma in my cooking. That's how she is in my life, and that's how she and I in turn stay alive. Memories and new adventures in the kitchen that I create keep my ma alive to me. It's said that it takes but one generation for family recipes, languages, and history to disappear—that's less than three decades. As long as I am here, my ma and baba will be too.

I continue to seek new foods the way Baba used to and to cook how Ma used to—stressing good clean flavors, spending as little time in the kitchen as possible, and always keeping my focus on the lively conversations around the dining table. The lamb curry I make is a version of Ma's, but I expedite the tenderization of the protein by marinating it in buttermilk. The flavor is enhanced by ground coriander, a ginger-and-garlic paste marinade, and tandoori masala to give the curry a rich color and zest. While my lamb curry may not have taken the route of bunny chow, created out of necessity and apartheid, the dish allows me to hold on to a world I know is gone, as a reminder of how I came to be.

DREAMING OF MA'S GOAT CURRY WHILE MAKING LAMB CURRY
···
Serves 4

For the marinade

2 pounds lamb shoulder
   (with bones)
4 tablespoons ginger-garlic
   paste
4 teaspoons jalapeno peppers

1 cup red onions
1 cup coriander leaves
   (fresh)
4 tablespoons tandoori
   masala powder

4 tablespoons ground
   coriander
2 teaspoons Kashmiri chili
   powder

2 teaspoons garam masala
1 ½ cups buttermilk
Salt to taste

Cut the lamb into 2- to 3-inch sized pieces (bone-in pieces may be larger). In a bowl, blend the remaining ingredients except buttermilk and mix well. Add the lamb pieces to the mix and coat well. Add the buttermilk to cover (adding more if needed) and chill in the refrigerator for a minimum of 1 hour.

For the curry

2 tablespoons grapeseed oil
   +2 tablespoons more, if
   needed
2 cups red onions (chopped)
2 teaspoons ginger-garlic paste
   in a 1:1 ratio
1 teaspoon green chilies
   (chopped, optional)
2–3 vine tomatoes, chopped
2 teaspoons coriander seeds
   (rough ground)

2 teaspoons garam masala
2 teaspoons Kashmiri chili
   powder
2 teaspoons tandoori masala
   (add more if you want more
   spice and flavor)
1 teaspoon fennel seed powder,
   set aside
2 teaspoons dry fenugreek
   leaves
Salt to taste

In a pressure cooker placed on a stovetop burner, heat the grape seed oil over medium heat. Add the onions, ginger-garlic paste, chilies, and tomatoes into the pressure cooker and cook till the oil separates from the tomatoes and the onions are slightly crispy and translucent. Mix the coriander, garam masala, cayenne, and tandoori masala in a small bowl and add the mix to the pressure cooker and continue to simmer. If needed, add 2 additional table-spoons of oil. Add the marinated lamb pieces and sauté. Add any remaining marinade from the bowl into the pressure cooker and cook on medium heat for 5–7 minutes. Add the fennel seed powder and stir well. Add more salt, Kashmiri chili powder, tandoori masala to taste and for color (the color of the lamb should be reddish brown). Add enough water to cover the lamb. Cover and pressure-cook the curry for 30 minutes on medium heat. Turn off heat and let the lamb cook as the pressure cooker cools. Once the heat is dissipated, the pressure cooker lid should open with ease. The lamb should be cooked through, with the meat falling off the bone in a stew-like consistency. Add more salt or tandoori masala to taste. With the lid off, place the pressure cooker on a burner and on low heat add the dry fenugreek leaves as needed to spice up the mix. Serve hot with basmati rice.

....

CHAPTER 5

When Indira Died
(Punjabi Tandoor)

One month after I turn fourteen, Indira Gandhi, the third prime minister of India and the first woman to govern the world's largest democracy, is assassinated in New Delhi.[1] Two days earlier, my ninth-grade civics teacher had warned us that he would be handing our class a test on gram panchayat election rules, those based on grassroots democratic governing councils at the village level. They made no sense to me and still don't. The assassination puts a halt to all education and life for nearly two weeks that autumn.

. . . .

It is October 31, 1984, a crisp, slightly chilly morning in New Delhi. There's a tinge of breeze in the Safdarjung Road garden separating the prime minister's bungalow from her offices. Indira Gandhi is sixty-six years old. She has short hair, a shock of white streaked at a favorable angle across the bob, making her striking, especially in election posters and *Times of India* caricatures. Her nose is long, her eyes fiery, her lips thin—all features we Indians have associated with those of Kashmiri pundits, just like her father, Jawaharlal Nehru, India's first prime minister. She has a thin but decisive voice and a fast walking pace. She carries a handloom jhola bag, though all her important files are with her secretary, R. K. Dhawan. He runs to keep up with the prime minister, who strides ahead in her orange handloom silk sari.

Documentary filmmaker Peter Ustinov is waiting to interview Indira in her office. He's making a movie about her. It is just after 9 a.m. Many important meetings have been scheduled by R. K. Dhawan so that Ustinov can film India's fiercest daughter at work—Indira, a woman who has led the world's largest democracy for a decade and a half.

Indira's security detail—five jawans, commando soldiers—are less than seven feet away. Among them are two Sikh bodyguards. Beant Singh, a twenty-five-year-old security elite and Indira's trusted bodyguard, stands near her. Satwant Singh, a twenty-two-year-old Sikh commando, exchanged his guard duty to be with Beant this morning instead of later that night. He too is close by, next to Beant.

"Namaste," she says, her last words, to Beant Singh.

He steps forward, a .38 pointed at her, "Bole so nihal, sat sri akal."

Whoever says these words is eternally happy, eternal is the Great Lord.

He pumps three bullets into her abdomen. From behind him, Satwant pulls his semiautomatic weapon, lodging thirty of thirty-three bullets in the sixty-six-year-old woman who is now crumpled on the garden path. Her jhola falls with her, her maroon blood staining her orange sari.

Both Sikh soldiers surrender to the other security guards.

Beant says, "I have done what I had to. You do what you have to."

In the guard offices, the two assassins are interrogated. Beant lunges for a security guard's gun. Satwant pulls out his kripan from his turban—the knife that every Sikh carries as part of their faith, to protect their religion. The guards shoot, killing Beant, critically injuring Satwant.

Ustinov's tape recorder records the screams of a dying woman. The world outside Safdarjung Road still doesn't know what has happened yet.

. . . .

Three months before this, in July 1984, Indira's cabinet ordered her not to have Sikh soldiers in her security detail.

She rejected that idea outright, saying, "When I have Sikhs like this

Punjabi kadhi

around me, then I don't believe I have anything to fear."[2] Indira had known Beant for many years. She trusted him with her life.

Hearing the shots, Indira's daughter-in-law, Sonia Gandhi rushes out, screaming, "Mummy, Mummy!"

Now the most important behind-the-scenes opposition politician in current India, but in 1984 still just an Italian-born daughter-in-law, Sonia gets her mother-in-law into the car. Cradling Indira's head in her lap, Sonia instructs the driver to move fast! Fast! The prime minister's assistant, R. K. Dhawan, accompanies the two women in the car, clutching the files, eyes on the road as the Ambassador speeds through New Delhi.

The prime minister's car drives the dying leader to the AIIMS Hospital in South Delhi, sirens blaring.

Indira's doctors attempt to revive a dead body for over an hour, with artificial lung and heart machines pumping eighty bottles of blood into a lifeless woman. At 10:50 a.m., an hour and a half after the bullets were fired, Indira is pronounced dead by the doctors. That news is released at 2:23 p.m. that day.

The war has only started.

. . . .

In the San Diego area, Punjabi Tandoor has three branches. The first one opened seventeen years ago in a small closet-sized space behind warehouses near Miramar Road, a middle-class neighborhood near Indian clothing and jewelry stores, an Indian bank, and a sorry little Hindu temple. The second branch opened almost a decade ago in a former sushi restaurant near Sorrento Valley, with a bank counter–like feel when you enter the cavernous open space. The third one opened in Carlsbad around the same time as the second, thirty miles north of San Diego in a strip mall, bustling with afternoon traffic from the biotech companies strewn around it. That's the one I visit almost regularly, despite the long line of lunch customers hungrily asking for chicken tikka, lamb curry, or saag paneer—fare that passes for Indian food in America.

The restaurant is run by Bakhtawar Saini, his brother, Jagdish Saini and their family. I've seen Bakhtawar's wife step in to assist when some of the younger assistants return to Jalandhar for their annual visit to Punjab. Bakhtawar's daughter, Satwinder has a perpetual smile, controls the cash register with grace, and speaks English with a slightly Americanized accent. In an in-your-face meat-centered Punjabi North Indian restaurant, she is a vegetarian who doles out chicken and lamb without judgment and without showing disgust at having to serve meat, even when the sauces slosh in the thin Styrofoam containers. Jagdish's nephew, Lucky, a tall skinny young man with a thick Sikh turban and thicker black beard, deftly handles the tandoor while fielding questions from the customers.

"Yes, lamb curry is spicy."

"Try the chole, it's really good today."

"Hey, man, haven't seen you forever, how've you been?"

His brown eyes smile every time I walk into the Carlsbad takeout restaurant, and silently he mimes, "Roti?" because it's not on the menu and I prefer the whole wheat roti to an all-purpose-flour, sticky naan. I usually nod, and Luis, his Mexican assistant, rolls out the wheat dough silently, handing it to Lucky so he can stick it to the side of the hot tandoori oven with his bare hands.

Lucky doesn't ask, "Chai?" because he knows and it goes without saying, I will never say no to tea. No self-respecting Indian will ever refuse tea.

I have been a regular at all the Punjabi Tandoors in San Diego for over seventeen years—the food hasn't changed. Neither has the service.

....

We are in our geography class in St. Anthony's Senior Secondary Girls' High School in South Delhi. It is almost noon. News isn't instantaneous in 1984 the way it is now.

Today, Mrs. Veena Singh, an army wife, who prefers to dress in soft georgettes and chiffons with pastel flowers, with her hair in a fashionable bob (even though she's a Sikhni), almost like Lady Di's, teaches us about monsoons, "This low pressure pulls this stream from the Australian side toward Southeast Asia."

Turning from the board and pointing at me, she says, "Madhushree, in what state does this hit India? West Bengal? Tamil Nadu?"

I stand up, brain frozen. Geography isn't my strong suit, even though Ma used to be a geography teacher. I clear my throat and pretend to think, "Miss, oh, um . . ."

Mother Pia, our principal knocks on the door. Relieved, I sit down promptly. The nun beckons the teacher outside.

They whisper with "No! What? No!" exclamations from Mrs. Veena Singh.

When Mrs. Veena Singh returns, Mother Pia adjusts her habit and tightens the rope belt around her jiggly belly, hidden under the white nun uniform. Her eyes sad, face round, Mother Pia announces to the class,

"Pray for Mrs. Gandhi, pray she gets better. Mrs. Veena Singh will be with you till the buses come. It's a sad, sad day. India's favorite daughter was shot. By her own bodyguards. Very sad, sad day."

We pray, being Catholic school students, we know the drill of asking Jesus for favors. When I peek at my teacher, Mrs. Veena Singh wipes her face with her sari, her pale cheeks now flushed red, crying.

Nandita, my best friend, and I point at our teacher—after all, teachers are supposed to make us cry, not the other way round. We are cruel teenagers, and any emotion that isn't loud and brash we perceive as weakness. Even though I actually like Mrs. Veena Singh very much, I cannot admit to that, especially when my friends giggle with a teenage bravado that is borderline mean-spirited.

We pack our bags, occasionally pulling each other's pigtails, unraveling the blue ribbons of St. Anthony's uniform dress code. Near the window, Mrs. Veena Singh stares into the street, unseeing. We are boisterous, but Mrs. Veena Singh doesn't stop us from talking loudly. We quieten down by ourselves. We don't know what else to do. She pulls her soft sari around her back, chewing on her lower lip that quivers involuntarily, her eyes watering.

Nandita nudges me, "Go ask her what's wrong."

As the class monitor, I don't have to ask for permission. But I ask for it anyway, "Ma'am, may I drink water from the faucet in the hallway?"

She waves me away, as if, "Do whatever you want."

I hesitate and stay. She looks up. Her eyes are brown, sad, foreign, "Do you know the Sikhni, the girl in eighth grade?"

Uh-huh, I say. I think her name is Simran—I'm not sure.

She is a Punjabi girl, two plaits, well-oiled braids, with a little sister in second grade or something. Studious, sweet, nothing spectacular. Long hair, serious face, the steel kara bangle on her right wrist, a sign that she is a Sikh.

Mrs. Veena Singh sighs, wiping the corner of her left eye with her lace handkerchief. She looks at me, "Well, her father was on the Rajdhani Express, the train coming to Delhi from Calcutta."

"Oh," I say, "How did you find out, Mrs. Singh?"

"Mother Pia told me. They can't reach him. It's afternoon. That train comes in early morning. He's a Sardar."

"Did she head home?"

She nods and squares her shoulders, as if bracing for an inevitable conflict, "He's a Sikh. Two Sikh soldiers shot at our prime minister. We aren't safe anymore."

The school bell rings, clanging us into attention. I look at Mrs. Veena Singh, helpless. I don't know who she means by "we." What's a fourteen-year-old to do? The only thing I can think of is whether the civics test will be canceled, since we're leaving school early.

"We aren't safe anymore." I hear the whisper again when I turn to pick up my bag from my chair.

. . . .

Jagdish Saini, Lucky's uncle, mans the cash register in Sorrento Valley. It is the pandemic after all, and the lunch crowd is sparse at best. Seeing me, he puts a white cloth over his white beard and nose, waving me in. His wife, in a pale-yellow rayon georgette salwar suit, quickly pulls her dupatta to cover her nose and mouth, head lowered.

"Welcome," he says, politely. His voice is soft, his eyes curious.

"Jagdish ji, I know your nephew, Lucky, from the Carlsbad store," I start awkwardly.

He stares back, polite but not helpful.

"I was wondering if I could talk to you about how you came here?"

"1986," he says, still polite, still unhelpful.

I think I might as well ask him what's on my mind. "So did you come here after the Hindu-Sikh riots?"

His eyes pierce into mine, but he doesn't say anything. I ask him again because I want to know.

He motions me to sit at a table near the counter. He clears his throat and sits across from me. Then, looking up again at me, Saini says, "That's personal. We don't talk about personal. We are religious Sikhs."

I don't have to ask him who he means by "we." He talks about his Sikh community. Near the cash register, a customer asks for extra saag paneer. His wife serves it on top of rice, quietly. Near her, a sign notes, "Good Vibes Only."

....

Four months before the day Indira died, she launched a military attack on the Sikhs' holiest temple, the Golden Temple.[3] There are many versions of this story. The one I know is this: According to the Indian government, the temple, the Mecca of the Sikhs, in the town of Amritsar, is taken over by terrorists. The demands of these men are for Punjab State to secede from India, to create Khalistan, the country of Sikhs.

Decades later, I find another version. Whom the government calls terrorists was debatable—Bhindranwale, an armed militant Sikh guru, talked about what being a true Sikh meant—his words were manna to Sikh young men, somewhat lost, trying to find their way.[4] He told them to be true Sikhs was to live in austerity, focus on faith, and live honest lives. His missionary zeal enabled the recruitment of many Sikhs into his religious group. These Sikhs were his trusted men, who defended Sikhism with zeal and, eventually, with militant power.

Sikhism started as a religion of peace in 1500 CE and was distinct from then prevalent Hinduism and Islam in its acceptance of other religions, the equality of men and women (reflected in their names being gender neutral), and their celebration of the Guru Granth Sahib, the holy text, rather than idols or a particular god. While the religious leaders did fight for their faith over centuries, Sikhs in general are known to be not just brave warriors but people of peace and faith. In the 1980s, Sikhs rose, asking for their rights for the first time, for the freedom to practice their religion, with AK-47s in their hands. Bole so nihal, sat sri akal.

Whoever says these words is eternally happy, eternal is the Great Lord.

....

Saini and I sit in uncomfortable silence for a few moments and I try again.

"So, you came here and started this restaurant?"

He shrugs, "No, I came here. But the community took care of us, my family. We've been in the restaurant business for years now."

I ask him how they decided what their menu should be. Saini's eyes light up.

"Well, this food is from our village. Saag paneer. Dal makhni—spiced lentils in butter and cream. Chicken tikka masala, chicken curry, and lamb curry. All that we eat at home."

"So you created your home in San Diego then?"

He smiles, finally. "Yes, comfort food, that's what we created for those who miss home. It's the same in all the three locations—have you tried them?"

Yes, I nod.

"Our food is truly comfort food, you know," he says, leaning forward. I see that this is what excites him: food, how he makes it, what he makes, and why. "It brings you back to where you came from. I've visited Italy. Germany. England. Now here. I ate Punjabi food everywhere. In Italy, I did eat Italian food for lunch; otherwise, only Punjabi food."

"I know. Indian food in London is very different from—"

"No," he interrupts, "the flavor remains the same."

I realize he isn't talking about recipes. He's talking about food that reassures. It doesn't really matter whether you add more garlic or an extra clove. It's the smell of the familiar that makes you want to eat that saag paneer, even if it isn't how your mother made it. It makes you feel like you belong.

"Come again," he invites me back, formally.

When I look back, the "Good Vibes Only" sign blinks back at me. I still don't know why Saini and his family moved here, but also, do I really want to know?

. . . .

In 1984, Indira's government considers them terrorists. Bhindranwale, the missionary terrorist with a bullet belt hung across his chest, tells the foreign press, "If Indira wants the Sikhs to live in Khalistan, we won't say no, but we'd like to live in India, as Sikhs.

That ambiguous statement sets off the war that destroyed a generation of Sikh youth. Did Bhindranwale tell the foreign press that he would lead Sikhs and Punjab out of India? Will a Sikh homeland of Khalistan be a separate country? Or did he say he was holding on to his faith and defending it with his AK-47?

Indira's government takes this as the Sikhs' call to secede. This is civil war. Bhindranwale and his loyal supporters, more than four hundred of them, now hunted, head to the Golden Temple, the Sistine Chapel of Sikhs, taking shelter.

June 1–10, 1984. The Indian Army—including commandos—storms the Golden Temple. This is done at the behest of Indira. In the dead of the night, foreign press journalists, waiting outside the temple premises, are whisked away by plainclothesmen into Haryana. When they return to the border, they aren't permitted to reenter Punjab.

Punjab is under a news blackout. What does trickle out is mostly unfounded, panicked tales and hearsay accounts, lies, or embellishments. To this date, the genocide of Sikh civilians in their temple hasn't been acknowledged by the world. The Indian army initially noted a death toll of eighty-three officers and soldiers and 554 Sikh militants and civilians. Unofficial records claim at least twenty thousand civilian and two thousand military casualties. The media blackout enables the dissemination of grossly exaggerated or reduced death toll numbers, all unverified.

Regardless, this much is true: in Operation Bluestar, ordered by Indira, the Indian army entered a religious place of worship, to kill civilians who had congregated at the temple to worship, alongside alleged terrorists.[5] Sikhs from all over the world are outraged.

When Bhindranwale is found with his trusted group, their bodies are riddled with bullets. Their photos plaster the *Statesman* and the *Times of India*. There is a bullet that passes through Bhindranwale's brain. Another through his eye. The photographs aren't censured or doctored. Every school-going child now knows that terrorists, holed up in the temple, were killed by the brave Indian army. This, too, is India, where newspapers splash the dead bodies like trophies, as if to show children what could happen if they wrong the government.

Then Indira dies. The Sikh assassins make sure the world knows that this is in revenge for Operation Bluestar—revenge for how their own were killed, the temple defiled, their holy texts destroyed in that mission. What comes next is worse.

. . . .

Ma's smile when she opens the door to our first-floor rental home is unexpectedly large. She doesn't hug us—we are Ghoshes after all. Physical demonstrations and professions of love are foreign to us. Instead, it was a word, a smile, a favorite dessert, perhaps even a long-sought-after Enid Blyton book, but never hugs or kisses. Certainly Ma never hugged me unless I hugged her first. Such displays in the Ghosh household were considered a sign of weakness.

On the day that Indira dies, Ma's smile lights up her face.

She says, sighing with relief, "Aaye, good, you two are back. Now shut the gate and then the door. We'll wait for Baba to come home."

Inside, the television blares the rapid-fire news in Hindi telling the world that Indira was shot by one of her own. Her son, Rajiv, a reluctant politician, is now the heir, the presumed prime minister. He says, "When a big tree falls, the earth shakes," referring to his mother and justifying the aftermath. Adjacent to him, Sonia hides behind her huge shades. The screen morphs in Congress party men screaming, "Khoon ka badla khoon!"

The revenge for blood is blood.

That evening, my favorite uncle and Baba's favorite brother, Shonajethu, arrives from the hillside town of Dehradun. He works for the UN and visits us every month.

Shonajethu worries, having seen this as a young man, "Now the violence will start. This is horrible. Just like Partition."

Partition. That word meant only one thing for most Indians when the British, before they left in 1947, divided India by religion, Muslim and

Hindu, into two nations, Pakistan and India. There was genocide then. It remains the largest human migration perpetrated by colonizers.[6] My parents, children then, walked, rode trains, bullock carts, and buses to get to the Hindu side of India. In 1984, they still talk about Partition as if it had just happened yesterday. Refugees once, refugees forever.

"But, but," I sputter, "Shonajethu, that's not true. This is between Sikhs and Hindus. Not the same."

Shonajethu, the most educated one in the family, his face a rounder and softer version of Baba's, shakes his head sadly, "Religion doesn't matter once revenge is in the air."

That evening, small pockets in Delhi erupt with stone throwing, people grieving Indira with loud wailing and chest beating, mourners all. The neighborhoods targeted by non-Sikhs are Sultanpuri, Mangolpuri, Trilokpuri—low-income areas in East Delhi and North Delhi, populated by Sikhs, refugees from what's now Pakistan.[7]

Baba goes to Market No. 1 to buy vegetables and fish. "There will be curfew soon, I know."

Ma's pleas of "Ogo, stop, we can live on potatoes and rice. Don't go!" fall on deaf ears.

The roads are quiet. Shonajethu leans next to the black-and-white TV screen, listening to the news loop over and over till all we hear is Indira's dead. Indira's dead. Indira's dead.

Baba returns with a few stalks of greens, okra, and eggplant.

Sighing, he tells us, "No fish, no chicken. The stores are shutting. The bread fellow, the Sardar is still there though—"

"Who, the Sikh?" I ask.

The Sikh sundries man—no, a boy maybe a few years older than us—manages a bread and eggs stall across the main street near the market.

Didi adds, "Doesn't he live in Kalkaji? Or is it Govindpuri?"

Those are the nearby Punjabi neighborhoods, where Sikhs and Hindus from Punjab moved into after Partition. Just like we Bengalis moved into Chittaranjan Park, Hindus all.

"Yes," Ma says, somewhat dismissive, "Govindpuri, I think. Na, maybe

Trilokpuri. He's stupid, not heading home. You need to save yourself, ego has no role to play."

Baba hands the grocery bags to Ma, silent.

Shonajethu calls his wife on the phone, "Yes, yes, I'm safe. I'll be here, don't worry."

Shonama screams at her husband on the other end of the line, "I told you not to go! They're killing people. I'm alone here."

Shonajethu sighs, defeated, "Ah, yes, but you're in the hills. Everything will happen in Delhi. I am sure they'll start a curfew soon."

. . . .

The first Sardar was killed the night Indira died.[8] In East Delhi. Then they said, no, that didn't happen. The first Sardar was killed the next day. By henchmen of politicians. In the neighborhoods where money is as scarce as water. Where Sikhs, with their beards and turbans, are easily recognizable. When the first death is reported, it is expected. We just don't know when the real "first" one is. Yet our family inhales in collective shock as the announcers report that on the state-run Doordarshan TV channel.

"Stay home," my uncle orders my father, who hates being confined inside.

Baba dismisses his brother, "Ah, really! Nothing will happen." But he doesn't leave either.

The next afternoon, we head upstairs to the terrace. I smell tires burning, rubber, wood; we see smoke. Downstairs, on our black-and-white TV, pictures flash. Indira's body rests ceremoniously in a state mansion, head covered in a sari, eyes closed, and dignitaries paying their respects.

On the terrace, Shonajethu says, "We'll all go to hell for this."

Baba says, "Yes, but they shouldn't have killed her, right?"

Shonajethu stops him, "Killing these people won't bring Indira back, will it?"

He points to the north. Ma strains her weak eyes in that direction and adds, "Look, look, smoke, hai bhogoban, smoke!"

Didi's eyesight is better than everyone else's. She points at another dark spiral in the distance, "Oi daykho, there, there's another one."

The city burns. Plumes of smoke rise from burning homes, neighborhoods are being destroyed. Later, we find out that Sikh men were pulled out of their homes, tires thrown on their necks. Kerosene poured on them by mobs. Lit matches thrown at them. Women chased down streets, raped, murdered, or let loose, walking zombies. Some—many—lose their minds. Children orphaned, wait near the destroyed lanes, looking for their parents. Politicians gave their henchmen the voter lists—they then marked doors of Sikhs, and when they returned with weapons, they targeted those doors. It was planned, easy, and predictable. Even now, there's a neighborhood called Widow's Colony—Sikh widows of 1984.

Hopefully, I ask Didi, "Then we can't go to school, na?"

Shonajethu replies instead, "You're happy your test is postponed, ki? The world is burning and you're happy your test is postponed, ki?"

I stick my tongue out at him. I do not comprehend the seriousness of death around me.

He then adds, "I hope you understand one day. Maybe not today, but someday."

We look at the dark smoke covering the skies.

. . . .

That night, police vans drive past our house, men announcing on the loudspeaker: "There's a curfew. Indira is dead. Stay inside."

Across the park from our house is the Punjabi neighborhood, Kalkaji. Hindu Punjabis and Sikh Punjabis. There's a Hindu temple next to a Sikh gurudwara. The next morning, we wake up to the sounds of "Bole so nihal. Sat sri akal."

On the other side, the sound of cymbals starting the Hindu prayer ritual, "Om jai jagdish hare, swami jai jagdish hare" percolates throughout the Bengali neighborhood.

Baba announces, "The Sikhs are saying they're ready with weapons in their temple."

Ma protests, "No, maybe all they're doing is praying."

"Dur," Baba dismisses Ma. "People thought even Bhindranwale was praying in the Golden Temple. See what he did, that terrorist?"

Ma is silent. Then she whispers to me, handing me a teacup for Baba, "Yes, but after they killed him, his people killed Indira, so it was all for nothing, na?"

"Yes, Ma," I say, even though, at fourteen, I'm not sure whether I'm to take sides in politics or at home.

Didi frets over her economics textbook, so Shonajethu sits next to her. Every time he gives her attention, she can concentrate, so he does. Baba gets in Ma's way in the kitchen, then he storms out of there when Ma protests. He then comes to the living room where I'm watching TV.

"Did they decide when the funeral is?"

"Tomorrow. Three days since she died," I assume, thinking the rituals were the same for a prime minister, but I wasn't sure.

"Yes, they can't keep a dead body like that. Brings bad luck. And temperatures in India—that just makes the body decompose faster. I hope they cremate her soon."

I watch Rajiv, Indira's sole surviving son, wipe his mother's brow as if she were alive. His two children, fair-complexioned like their Italian mother, sit quietly, obediently on the floor next to their dead grandmother. Politicians from all over the world come to pay their respects, with soft sitar music playing in the background. Placing rose and gardenia wreaths, they bow their heads. Then they look around, uncertain, unfamiliar with Hindu customs, afraid to commit a religious faux pas.

Then they announce on TV, "We expect more violence, so please stay at home. Police have shoot-at-sight orders."

We are stuck in our house. All we have left is rice and potatoes.

Ma says mournfully, "No fish or meat. We are on a widow's diet."

I'm glad the civics test is canceled.

. . . .

In 2012, a white supremacist attacks a Sikh gurudwara in Oak Creek, Wisconsin. Six Sikh granthis are killed. Their names end with Singh, they appear foreign. The nation offers prayers and thoughts.

Afterward, the Sikhs welcome everyone to their langar, the communal kitchen—it's kar seva, which literally translates to "service with your own hands," meaning, to welcome everyone to a free meal prepared by the Sikhs in the gurudwara. They focus on what their religion teaches them. Violence as a last resort. Till then, love. Only love.

. . . .

Late evening, goons from the ruling party—Indira's party—head to the Punjabi neighborhoods. Their bosses, politicians ruling the country, arrive in government-issued cars with tinted windows. They hand out voter lists with bottles of alcohol as bribes. With lists in hand, the goons walk through the tight lanes where only bicycles can pass and mark an S on doors that protected Sikh families. That night, alcohol in most of their bellies, with curfew imposed, the same groups of men are dropped off at different main roads leading to small lanes with S symbols on old, cracked doors. They pull families out on the streets, strip the men of their turbans, pull down their pants because they can, light their beards on fire. Their wives, mothers, sisters run to their spouses, sons, brothers, fathers, and are dragged to corners of alleyways. Their fate is worse, they are left to live. People are burnt, children killed. The police, vans in tow, bullets in their rifles, turn a blind eye. New Delhi burns and Sikhs die. India's fiercest daughter was killed. This is war. This is revenge.

Middle-class families like mine get used to curfew. Baba goes early morning to buy milk and bread. The Sardar's sundries shop has been set on fire, Baba says.

He adds, "I hope he's alive—poor boy. He didn't do anything. I think he's the only earning member in his family."

Shonajethu nods. "Yes, let's hope the killings stop. I'm glad you agree too, Hashi."

Baba nods, taking a drag on his cigarette, "I wasn't saying, kill them. But no one should ever think they can kill the prime minister. That's all."

Ma interrupts. "I just want my daughters to go back to school. People are dying, people are illiterate, what kind of society is this? You two need to leave India for America as soon as you get out of college, bujhli?"

Didi and I head to the front verandah and stare at the empty park in front. The air still smells of smoke, of burnt, dead Sikhs. We are used to an abnormal situation—it doesn't even take us a week to adjust.

In the distance, we see a group of young men, men from the neighborhood shanty homes, heading on the road from Greater Kailash toward us. The men in '70s bell bottoms and the floppy hair of present-day Bollywood actors, men with no education, these men walk on the road separating us. Us, the middle class, from them, the riffraff, as Ma calls them.

Sidling close, Didi pulls her shawl around herself and pokes me from underneath the red wool, "Chol, let's go in. We need to head inside."

"Na, Didi, c'mon, don't you see these fellows? See, see!"

"Don't be stupid. You don't know if they have knives or guns."

I laugh at my seventeen-year-old sister's fears. I ask her, "What will they do? Throw the knife at us? Haven't you studied projectile motion in school, Didi? It'll never reach us, and those idiots don't have good aim, they look like losers."

"Why do you want to see them, eh?" Didi's question stops me.

I don't know why I want to see them. I am curious, and that's all I know. The men, three, maybe four of them, have jars in their hands, two per person, large glass jars, with metal lids.

Baba walks out of the living room, hearing us. "Ki?"

"Baba, those men stole jars from a grocer's shop. Na?"

Baba nods, "Yes, shala, chor—robbers! I've seen them. Where, oh, yes, the Sardar's shop. He's the only one with steel covers, the other grocers have regular plastic jars."

The first man, with a Jeetendra floppy haircut doesn't notice us. The second one, darker, eyes flashing, looks up. His hand is in the jar he carries.

He fondles the purple covers of three Cadbury chocolate bars. Turning to the third man in the group, he says, "Here, take one."

The third man, a boy really, his polyester shirt with brown flowers sticking to his thin torso asks, "Really? Kitne, how many, eh?"

"Don't know, four, five."

The second man, his green shirt fluorescent, black pants now dusty, stares up at us, no expression on his face, hand still in the jar.

Baba leans over the railing, "Ai, kahan se uthaya? Where did you get the chocolate from, you good-for-nothing?"

Green Shirt glowers, "What's it to you, old man? Mind your own business."

It's the first time I hear my father being called an old man. I leap into the conversation, "Shut up, you idiot, you thief. Stealing things because you're a lying thief!"

I realize I don't say anything. It's in my head that I am a hero.

Baba yells again, "You stole it from Sardar's store. Bhagvaan will curse you, his god and yours, you luffunga good-for-nothing."

Shonajethu stage whispers from behind us, "Hashi, stop talking to low-class people. They stole from the Sikh. They'll attack you next. Come inside."

Inside, Baba seethes, inhaling his cigarette like it's an oxygen mask.

Ma lectures from the kitchen, "Yes, go, go, fight the low-class people. They'll kill you just like they killed Indira and the Sikhs. Go on, you brave people, go, join the fight."

Near the flickering lamp post, the men distribute the Cadbury's chocolate, tearing the foil wrapper with a greediness I had rarely seen. Brown Flowers boy opens his two jars—both filled with gold coins—chocolate discs wrapped in gold foil. He opens a few, one by one, and takes one bite from every one of them. As if his bite imprints ownership—even though he stole them.

The first man, with Jeetendra's haircut, looks up. His eyes glower through the white plumeria tree, sizing me up and down. I take a step back and bump into Didi.

Didi whispers, "Let's go. Don't stand there."

As I move away slowly, heading to the TV, Jeetendra bites into the chocolate bar, as if chocolate is the only thing that will satisfy him.

Later, when I look outside, there is no one.

From then on, Baba starts to lock the gate and the door leading to our upstairs home.

. . . .

Indira is cremated with a 21-gun salute against the background of plaintive shehnai music. Mourners cry loudly along the way. Her family leads the group. There's no mention of the Sikhs killed, the missing people. No one is jailed for stealing chocolates or the lives of others.

In two weeks, we return back to school. Shonajethu heads to his home in the hills, and his wife makes him promise never to leave her alone.

Two weeks after Indira dies, Baba returns to the bank, busies himself with his accounting ledger books and constant phone calls to customers. He continues to lock the gate till we move out of that rental in B Block to our own home, my mother's dream house in Pocket 40, C. R. Park. He locks the gate in the new home too, till he dies and Ma takes over.

Two weeks after Indira dies, Didi takes her economics exam and I have my dreaded civics test—I get an eight out of ten, but Ma doesn't scold me, so we pretend that test never happened. Even today, civics is still a subject that can lull me to sleep in seconds.

Mrs. Veena Singh returns. Her georgettes still sparkle, but not her eyes.

The next March, with the new school year, Mother Pia tells us, "Oh, Mrs. Veena Singh's army husband got transferred to Chandigarh. She's gone."

The Sikhni and her little sister keep to themselves during recess. They eat their parathas near the biology lab steps.

Nandita tries to get her to join us, "C'mon, let's hang out!"

No, the Sikhni shakes her head, holding her sister's hand. They leave politely, quietly. Next year, I find out that their mother took them to Canada or someplace foreign. They never find her father's body. He was pulled out of the Rajdhani Express that morning in October. He was handsome and brave, according to the nuns of St. Anthony's.

·············

Ma lets us go to Market No. 1 by ourselves to buy milk, bread, and eggs. I hear the Sardar is back.

I ask Didi, "What'll he sell from that burnt store?"

Didi says, "You're evil, Rumjhum. He needs business. I'll buy the bread and eggs if he's selling. Got it?"

Uh-huh.

We cross the main road. The Bengali neighborhood bustles again, fish-walas yell out: Bhetki! Katla! Magur! from their stalls, a catalog of the fish in their baskets.

Mukim, our Muslim halal meat man, cleans his long knife slowly, splashing water rhythmically. Next to the milk depot, the mishtiwalas heat up the oil to fry the jalebis, flicking the flies away with a dirty rag tied to a stick, expertly maneuvering the fried dough squiggles into a sticky sugar syrup stationed precariously near the hot burner. The air is still warm this winter. We wear sweaters regardless because we're Bengalis and the one thing we're worried about is catching a cold in Delhi.

I never noticed how young the Sikh is till I see him that day, over a month after Indira died. Everyone gapes at him, like it's the circus. No one has seen someone's world so completely destroyed by anger. The storefront has a black gash of smoke where looters threw in a kerosene bomb. His shelves are mostly empty, just a few bread loaves and two racks of eggs. The glass jars with metal lids are missing. Instead, there are four small plastic jars with red lids—each filled with two packets of Parle-G biscuits.

I look at him: his eyes are wet, his gray shirt torn. His turban is still intact, but grimy, as if that's the only one he has to wear every day. He's a boy, whereas the others who stole the Cadburys were all men.

He wipes his eyes when someone asks him what happened.

The Sikh shakes his head and says, "How can I help you?"

Didi steps up, "Brother, we need one Modern bread and six eggs please."

He nods, hands her a loaf wrapped in a waxed paper with red and blue checks and "modern" written in ugly stylized letters. Packing six eggs in a flimsy newspaper bag, he holds his hand out for the money. I give him a note. He touches it on his forehead, the universal sign of "thank you."

I take the eggs and whisper, "Thank you, bhaiya."

The Sardar nods, his watery eyes still not meeting mine, "Thank you, sister."

．．．．．．．．．．．．．．

Lucky texts me six weeks into quarantine. *How are you?*

Good, you?

Business is slow, but that's expected.

I'd love to order but need home delivery. It's too far for you to come over to drop off some kadhi chawal, right?

He replies almost instantly. *Not far at all.* It's as if he needed an excuse to do the things that used to be normal a few months ago.

He arrives with a plastic bag of roti, Punjabi kadhi, and spinach paneer. In another small container is the famous lamb curry that only Punjabi Tandoor can make. He hands it over the gate, his beard covered in a mask, his eyes still shiny with joy.

"Not much we can do," he shrugs, "God will take care of us, one way or the other. Right now, we have to control the virus."

I tell him my diagnostics theory. It's still early in the pandemic, and we are still hopeful that life will get back to how it was in January. We still haven't seen those numbers climb up the way they do three weeks after that.

"Wear a mask and wash your hands. When it's fall, this will stop."

He's a young man, and as young men often are, he's carefree. "Achcha ji, it'll be fine, whatever it is." Climbing down the steps, he waves, "Take care!"

I tell him to be safe and give my regards to Kamaljeet, his wife. I hope to see him soon in the little takeout store in Carlsbad. On social media, I write about the Sainis—that their food has sustained me for days. That they feel like family even though I hardly know them and they, me. Lucky presses a heart on that post.

Later the next month, deaths in San Diego creep up. The toll is not as high as New York, but creep up they do. I thicken kefir with chickpea flour, a dash of turmeric with ginger and cumin. I sauté a few potato pakoras and add the yogurt mixture. I season it with a chaunk of cumin and mustard seeds along with a dash of asafetida. The spice mix sputters when added to the yogurt-pakora bowl. Eating the kadhi with rice and my homemade roti, I still long for the kadhi from Punjab Tandoor. It sure is comfort food, made by people who know what home used to be.

CHAPTER 6

....

Dessert in Kolkata Summers
(Search for Naru)

If it was a trip to Kolkata, it was always to our large penthouse-like condominium where Baba's entire joint family lived. Summer break, Didi and I piled into the train from New Delhi to Kolkata, Ma clutching her purse and our hands for dear life, Baba waving at us from the platform, saying, "Have fun, aami aashbo in two weeks to bring you all back."

But he'd turn away even before the train pulled out, a cigarette dangling from his lips, his thoughts already focusing on the bank, the loans, and all things work.

I remember our 1982 Kolkata trek. I was giddy with excitement because we were going to hang out with our favorite cousin, Didibhai. She's a decade older than me and therefore wiser. She had started her new job as a math teacher in St. Thomas' Day School, teaching mainly poor Christian and Muslim children, and tried to look older than her twenty-two years by wearing her mother's saris to school.

The first day, we headed after lunch to our other cousin's house. Minudi lived in a middle-class neighborhood called Gariahat, close to the sari shops and fresh vegetable markets when supermarkets were still foreign to us.

Ma told Didibhai, "Don't be late, and hold your sisters' hands tightly."

Didibhai hugged her tightly instead.

Ma bore the hug with a grimace, waiting for it to stop.

Didibhai calmed her down with an "Of course, these are my little sisters, of course I'll take care of them. We'll have tea at Minu-di's house and
be back by evening, okay?"

By the time the bus pulled into the Jadavpur bus stop where we waited,
it was full. There were people spilling out of the bus, holding on to the
door jamb or latching a foot on the last step, like a suitcase filled with
clothes, with errant socks, a T-shirt or two, or a shoe sticking out of the
half-closed box. That kind of full. Didibhai pushed us in, with a "Chol,
chol, get inside, quick!" We didn't argue with her, she knew what to do.

We got off at the fourth stop. The conductor helped me get down.

Didibhai glared at him and said, "Oh ho, don't be so chivalrous, helping
a little girl get down, you dirty horny bastard!"

Didibhai knew her way around, and the meek-looking bus conductor
looked down shiftily. I didn't really think he was trying to put his hand up
my skirt, but hey, what did I know? I was twelve, from Delhi, and wearing
a dress to see my older cousin after many years. Didi was as street-smart
as Didibhai, as she reminded me often. I assumed I had to listen, being the
youngest, therefore most naïve and ultimately the most clueless.

Minu-di was at the verandah watching us walk toward her place.

"Aha! Who is it? The two little Ghosh girls, I see, eh?"

Minu-di in 1982 may have been in her forties, but to me she looked
ancient. She reminded me of Baba's favorite sister, Pishimoni, the same
wavy hair, the same gait, but a couple of sizes smaller than her. Pishimoni
was the aunt I hated with a vengeance for no reason but that Ma said that
Pishimoni was very sad when Baba married Ma. That reason, to me, was
reason enough. Besides the physical similarity, Minu-di wasn't hateable at
all—she had soft brown eyes that were always full of love. Her sari was
a thin cotton, as if she didn't have money to spare, but the house was colonial, with tall ceilings, long columns, white pillars, and solid red steps
leading to an enormous front room. To me, it reeked of a sad, sagging
wealth that was long gone. When I spoke with Didi recently about Minu-
di's house, she didn't recollect it the way I did—she thought the room was
a midsize one and there were no columns. But then, this is the trickery of

Naru

memory, because that afternoon Minu-di's front room seemed enormous, the steps were a deep red, the columns were tall, and the sun was relentless.

"Minu-di, ki shundor baari," Didi exclaimed, looking around appreciatively like Ma would when she visited neighbors. Didi used words that adults would, nodding, peering as if to notice details carefully, much like Ma.

"I love those cane chairs, so lovely!"

Minu-di waved her comment away, "Ah, all old stuff, your aunt's, my mother's furniture."

At fifteen, Didi who knew big words, announced, "Ah, antiques, eh?"

Minu-di giggled, and hid her tiny teeth behind her tiny palm, "Teek, teek, whatever you say!"

She went to the kitchen while we sat on the overstuffed sofa and admired the woodwork on the sofa arm.

"Kashmiri carving work," Didibhai informed me. "It's teak, very expensive."

"Ah," Didi and I exclaimed, impressed.

Minu-di came out of the kitchen in the back with a tray. Mishti: soft balls of paneer with cardamom mixed with date palm jaggery; naru, coconut balls rolled in fresh date jaggery; savory chickpea-flour fried sticks; and three bone china cups filled with the sweetest Nescafé I've ever had. She may have added ten spoons of sugar per cup. In 1982, I didn't know I could say no to sugary drinks. In fact, I think I liked sugary drinks then, so why would I say no to it? Instant coffee was the only coffee I knew of, so that cup of sugary Nescafé was the most perfect drink I ever had.

Didibhai and Minu-di discussed our aunts, our uncles, Ma, and Baba. They talked about weddings, deaths, and births. They gossiped about the very loose cousin who was now living in sin with this man who didn't seem to have a job but had a lot of money. Didi hung on to every word, and I wandered from room to room, catching phrases like "in sin, in sin I tell you!" or "if only we had money to repair the water tank," followed by "bhaari sweet, very pretty daughter-in-law."

. . . .

November 2011.

In 2011, I am the technical head of a biotech company, B——, based in San Diego. That November, I represent the company at a meeting with the Food and Drug Administration in Washington, DC.[1] The meeting is standard protocol, confirmed by both groups, for the company to ask the FDA for approval of a new point-of-care instrument. The new device could detect multiple respiratory viruses, such as the flu, pneumonia, respiratory syncytial virus, and mycoplasma in less than an hour from a nasal swab. Small enough to be placed in doctors' offices, in Walgreens or CVS pharmacies, the instrument was expected to change how quickly patients could be diagnosed and treated. In 2011, the device, smaller than a minifridge, is a game changer—a game changer that needed FDA approval before the company could sell it to clinics, hospitals, and pharmacies.

The FDA is close to the Maryland university where my now ex and I met a decade and a half ago. I take the red-eye from San Diego. I am tired, the team is excited, nervous—this will be a make-or-break time for the company. I square my shoulders and ignore my sore back—the pain in my body is like an alarm clock I am ignoring, and I have been for a decade and a half. The meeting will be for the FDA to tell us whether we're on the right track to make a diagnostic test that will help healthcare workers diagnose diseases accurately and quickly. It is what patients need.

When I reach the hotel, I calm my team down—they have been slaving away at the presentation all night in the hotel suite. "We've worked hard to get here. The FDA will know we're experienced, and our product speaks for itself. Okay?"

The team nods. Behind them, the instrument whirs quietly in the hotel suite. "Madhu, what if it stops during the demo to the FDA?"

I shake my head confidently, "I trust you. You guys know this better than anyone else, relax."

The engineers go back to staring at the code on the screen. A message pops up on the screen noting that the DNA from the swab is ready to be amplified through a polymerase chain reaction. It's standard operating procedure for me—this is what I've done for decades in lab now. Nothing new to see. The team has it under control.

I tell them, "I'm going to my room for a bit. See you in an hour."

At check-in, I ask for a quiet room. That year is the year my now ex spends every two weeks refusing to talk to me for some reason, any reason. Sometimes it's because I added too much oil to the greens, sometimes it's because I bought couscous instead of quinoa. Sometimes it's because I don't want to have children. Sometimes it's because I have a job and he's had to compete for my attention. Sometimes he seems miserable to be with me. Most times, I am miserable to be with him.

The day before I had to head to DC, my now ex shouted at me—I don't remember now what for. It doesn't matter. What matters is that I knew he wouldn't talk to me for days. And I was leaving, so I calculated the countdown for when he'd talk to me again—since I wasn't going to be home, perhaps he'd talk to me when I returned? Perhaps he'd forget his need for me to be present when he withdrew his affection and communication? That's what I thought I could look forward to—that I could go to DC, stay the few days needed for work, come back, and he'd be ready to talk to me again.

When I take the red-eye to DC, I am looking forward to landing and heading to the hotel bed. All I want to do is sleep because I cannot sleep in my own house. I did not know in 2011 that this cyclical life of rage, anger, and simmering silences isn't how a Ghosh daughter is to be treated. I didn't know—I thought this is what marriage is meant to be, so I played my part in this misery. We stayed unhappy and yet together, neither one of us naming this unhappiness as anything because if we named it, we'd have to face it. I wasn't ready to be alone. I didn't know then what alone really meant.

2011. It is the first time I ask myself, "How do I start over again? Who will believe me?"

All everyone sees is a beautiful couple—two people who love each other, who finish each other's sentences. Who will believe this unbelievable, horrible dread I feel every day I return to the home we share?

2011. We have a routine without articulating it. I live in the bedroom, he in the living room. From the large TV out there, he hikes up the volume to the Tennis Channel. Inside, I watch E! These are different worlds, different visions. The irony of what we're expressing to each other isn't lost at all; we are tied to each other because we don't know what else to do if we weren't. Silence is what keeps us together. If we spoke, we wouldn't be.

....

1982. It was midafternoon after all, and I was sleepy. The naru was sweet, and the coffee was sweeter. And it was the coffee that made me look for the bathroom. I wandered around the house some more. Walking down the front steps, I peeked through a slightly ajar door.

I opened it. Ah, yes, it was a bathroom. It was next to the front steps from the street to the house. A peculiar place to have a bathroom, almost on the street. As if some fellow walking up the street might climb the steps and decide, "Oh, let me pee in a stranger's house for no reason but that it's right here."

Regardless, coffee. I went in, locked the door. It had the same red polished cement floor that will be popular in 2020, but then it was just an old bathroom. The shower area was separated by a half wall. The toilet was a floor one, an Indian style that I was used to but that we didn't have in our home in Delhi, so it was fascinatingly quaint. When I finished, I looked toward the half wall, and I swear I could feel someone watching me.

....

Inside the Hilton, I drag my suitcase into my room, place the cellphone on the charger, head to the bathroom. When the water from the faucet sprinkles my face, I look up and notice new creases, worry lines near my eyes.

I have been with my now ex for over a decade and a half. I am still the unsure, unconfident young girl from India, in love, in fear, in disarray. I have wrinkles to prove that something happened in those years. Nothing magical. Nothing pretty. A decade and a half of worry that he'll abandon me. A decade and a half of me being too much of a bossy woman. A decade and a half of us arguing, then making up, him throwing things against the wall, the floor, the sink, the door, but he never hits me. A decade and a half of him making silly jokes that make me laugh so much that I cry. A decade and a half of me cooking new things, old recipes, his favorites, just to see that smile on his face. That decade and a half is on my face. I splash more water. The FDA meeting is important. I have to focus.

I turn the knob. The door is locked. I didn't lock it. The lock seemed loose when I shut the door, and now it's jammed. From the bathroom, I hear the phone ring. Didi. She's calling me to check whether I reached DC. Yes, Didi, I did. I jiggle the handle. I cannot open it. I panic. I hate small places. Small rooms. The exhaust in the bathroom whirs loudly. This is funny, I tell myself aloud.

"This is funny, Madhushree Ghosh!"

I yell out, and my tired reflection is not brightened by the flecks of water from the splashing that decorate my black sweater like diamonds.

"You are locked in, Dr. Ghosh," the reflection says.

"You're locked in. In your life. In your work. You're locked in," the reflection mocks.

Claustrophobia makes one sharp and paralyzed all at once. I am all those things. I call out, "Help!"

"I am in room 718, help!" I scream through the air vent above the bathtub.

"Dr. Ghosh," my reflection still mocks me. "You chose the quiet room. You chose. It's been your choice all along. Love. Life. Work. Your choice, Dr. Ghosh."

The Hilton bathroom is a bunker. Bunker, my mind laughs. This isn't a war. What happens at home has entered my life outside. I am stuck in a bathroom for work. This is such a story! The walls are thick with slabs of granite guarding the bathtub, the sink. One wall faces the front façade, so it's a fort. The other wall, wall-papered a pleasant noncommittal beige faces the hallway.

I scrape the wallpaper, sheet by sheet. My nails scratch through the thick glue.

"Help!" I scream, my voice now old, hoarse.

The plaster falls off. I pull it again. The grit along with the white powdered pieces crumbles.

....

I know what you're thinking. Some weird crazy person was in the bathroom since it was close to the steps near the front entrance of that house. Or you're thinking, this is a ghost story. But this is what happened in 1982. Did I hear something? Yes, I did. Did I see something? Yes, I did.

But you know when you're in that moment, you don't know what's up and what's down. Also, I was twelve, with a vivid imagination.

The interesting part of someone watching you is that it's a feeling one can't really explain. Except that there is an intense awareness, and you have to turn around to check who's trying to get your attention. But I was twelve. So I didn't. I focused on washing my hands. The mirror on the wall had black spots where the paint chipped off over time. Through that, I looked again behind me, the half wall separating the water container from the rest of the bathroom.

I can't stay here anymore, this is too much to bear.

The voice was raspy, like Rani Mukherjee's. Young, like a new actress's earnest lilt. I swear I heard those words. She spoke in Bengali. I heard the words come from behind the half wall. There was a crack in that sentence, like she really couldn't bear it.

Aami aar paarchina. I can't bear this anymore.

Should I have looked up? Should I have stayed? No. No. No.

I didn't wait. Struggling with the latch, I said my Hail Marys as if I were the Catholic I used to pretend to be in school. The latch gave, then stuck. The door creaked as if it were sagging with sorrow. I was still in the bathroom and the sadness of that voice was enveloping me like an unnatural fog in Kolkata.

....

The wallpaper is off. I have placed it neatly in the bathtub; I don't want the housecleaning folks to be inconvenienced when they clean the room later. I assume there's a later. I run the water and drink from the faucet. I cannot panic. I start again. My right wrist hurts from banging against the wall. I use my left hand.

Help. Help.

The insulation is next. I move the tufts of fiber. I choke, I pull again, gusts of cotton, chemicals, wool-like globs come off. I try not to breathe. Analytical me laughs.

"The place has aerosoled carcinogens, Dr. Ghosh. How long will you hold your breath? Will you hold it for fifteen years like you have with him? How long will you hold on? How long will you take this?"

I pull out the last insulation. The air is smoky with particulates. Dr. Ghosh, PhD, in nickel-mediated carcinogenesis.

. . . .

The door had a heavy iron latch. It wasn't that easy to open, especially for a petrified me. It's not that the woman behind the half wall walked to me. It's not that she said anything else. All I felt was her soft sadness, if that's what it was. Her grief enveloped that bathroom. I had to leave. The lock stuck, I jiggled it, fear making every movement of mine slow, clumsy.

By the time I stumbled up the steps, the bathroom door awkwardly banging shut behind me, I screamed with every step I took up the stairs to the main house. "Didibhai, Didibhai, ghost, bhoot, ghost, shit, we gotta go now!"

Running toward me, Didi yelled, "You okay? All good? Did you fall asleep?"

"No, stupid. I went to pee. There's someone in that bathroom. She's not happy and sounded sad. But there was no one. It's a fucking ghost!"

(I knew bad words in English like fuck that I learned in Catholic school. I used them fluently with Didi—it made us seem cool.)

From the dining table, Minu-di got up, a look of concern in her eyes. "Which bathroom did you go to?"

"The downstairs one."

"The one near the steps?" she asked softly.

"Yes, that's the only one, no?"

She inhaled a sharp breath, shook her head. Then she rushed to the puja room, coming back with incense. Her cotton sari pallu wafted behind her like a soft mist. She hovered the stick over my head, muttering Sanskrit verses I was unfamiliar with.

Didibhai seemed serious, but she was the only one who could tell us what really happened. So I asked her, "Didibhai, what happened? What's going on?"

"No one goes into that bathroom," she said quietly. As if that would explain everything.

"You never told me. And why don't they—?"

"Because Toton-di died there."

"Who?"

"Toton-di," Didibhai said softly, looking sideways at Minu-di, to see whether she had offended her.

I didn't even know I had another cousin, a dead one at that.

"Why did she die there? Did she slip and fall?"

Minu-di shrugged with a "Ja geh, it's okay, so glad you came, I should lock that bathroom. And not let anyone go in there. It's a place of sadness."

Didibhai ushered us out saying, "It's late. Their mother will worry, we'll see you later, Minu-di! Thanks for the coffee."

I added, even though I was confused, but I added this anyway, because Ma had taught us to thank the hostess when we left, "Thank you for the naru, Minu-di."

. . . .

In a few weeks I will be at a face-to-face interview at G—— company, interviewing for a position three levels higher than the one I have here. The interviewer, an engineer with a solid instrumentation background, will peer at my resume. "What's your PhD on, Dr. Ghosh?"

I will answer, "My work focused on how metals like nickel and cobalt—"

"You mean, metals we have in currencies? Coins?"

"Yes, and some of it is in coal mining, and some, believe it or not, in beer."

"Beer? Really?"

"Yes, in the metal vats that beer is stored in. We found this English village near coal mines where their miners had a high proportion of lung cancer in the seventies."

"That's a cancer cluster," the engineer will announce, adjusting his round-rimmed glasses.

"Yes," I will continue because he understands. "The beer vats in the village pub were found to have cobalt and nickel impurities. That was my thesis."

Looking puzzled, the engineer will say, "You mean that beer had metal impurities? That doesn't make sense."

I will rush to explain, "No, no. My thesis covered the research on how cobalt, which was an impurity, along with nickel in these beer vats entered the coal miners' bodies. The metals also entered their lungs through the coal they mined—the carbon had cobalt and nickel as impurities in those mines."

The expression in his eyes will be of incredulity. Like this is a sci-fi story. But the engineer will not stop me.

"The miners' bodies recognized the metals as 'attacking agents'—and tried to block or encapsulate the foreign attacking bodies. I showed how those chemical bonds of metals linked with DNA building blocks, guanine and cytosine. The metal encapsulation led to tumors; the DNA mutated, leading to cancer."

Pushing his round-framed glasses again, an unconscious tick, the engineer will smile awkwardly, the way only introverted people can. He will offer, "That's amazing work, Dr. Ghosh. Tell me, what music do you listen to?"

"No, music distracts. Especially when I'm working. When I'm not, I turn to NPR."

The engineer will nod approvingly.

Across from him, the chief medical officer, who is to be my boss, will nod slightly, her eyes impenetrable. I will know that she will realize then that she has found a loyal worker. One who will not falter, will not be distracted. I will know then that I have this job. I know I have it.

. . . .

On our way to the bus stop, Didibhai, her eyes serious, told us this, "Toton-di committed suicide."

"What? Why? Who? When? Why?"

"We don't know. She was beautiful. She had the thickest hair, she looked like Zeenat Aman. She used to wear scandalous spaghetti strap blouses with her saris when even the Bollywood actresses didn't. She got offers to model, but she only wanted to be a teacher."

"So, why . . . ?" Didi tugged at Didibhai's arm.

"No one knows. They think someone in the family did something to her. She couldn't bear it."

"Who? Minu-di was mean to her?"

"No, her brother."

I couldn't keep track of how many other cousins I had, so I gave up. Which brother, who, why? And what bad things?

. . . .

Three hours later—I know because I still am wearing Baba's watch, the one with Russian lettering, given by a satisfied client a hundred years ago— I reach the final wall.

"Help me, please." I whisper to no one.

The watch dial now has white specks from the wall covering it unevenly. I've been in this fancy bunker of a bathroom, in a fancy hotel in the quiet part of DC—a room I specifically asked for. No one can hear me, maybe because no one expects me to scream. I chose this room. I chose him, my now ex.

Why would I be screaming for help? I shouldn't. I shouldn't be asking for help. I am strong. I am powerful. I am confident. I chose my path. I chose this place.

I reach the final wall. It separates me from the Hilton hallway and freedom. All I have to do is scrape that off with the metal tissue holder.

Through the torn wallpaper and drywall, I reach the electrical wires. Cables and cables of them, some tied together, some free-floating, different colors, muted in the dark hollow of the hotel innards. I give up—metal on wire is not a good combination, Dr. Ghosh, my grimy reflection mocks from the other side. Not a good combination.

I feel I am hallucinating. I talk to my then husband.

"You and I, we aren't a good combination. We think we are. We shine bright together. We love that we look good together. We're not a good combination."

I am also not the dramatic kind. But talking to him in this tiny bathroom on the East Coast somehow feels right. I know he can't hear me. But I need to say those words. We are not a good combination. I breathe the particulates in the air.

"Enter me, particulates, aerosols, carcinogens, will you, I am done, I am done. Help me," I whisper.

In the far distance, through an echo-y hollow I hear a "Hello? Hello? Who's there? Hello?" An older man, speaking broken Chinese-accented English.

"Here, here, I'm in 718. I'm trapped."

"Why don't you just open the door, lady?" The voice sounds very confused—it should be simple to just open the door, right?

I laugh. Relief washes over, "I would sir, if I could! Help!"

He's on the walkie-talkie calling for back up. Then he returns to the hallway separating me and him, with a question that's clearly bothering him, "Why you put the lock on, lady?"

"Because I'm a woman, and we always lock the hotel room doors as soon as we get in. "I wasn't expecting to be locked inside, dude! C'mon, I'm claustrophobic!"

"Oh," he says, shutting up.

His partner shows up.

"Ma'am?" It's a different, younger voice.

"Yes?"

"Could you please stand in the bathtub? I'm going to kick the door open, and I don't want to hurt you."

I climb into the debris in the bathtub. I think of telling my now ex about this incident. Then I remember we aren't talking to each other. I don't know when I will, next. In the next couple of weeks? In the next month? Two? Never? But I know he will never know what I heard inside this bathroom.

If I get out, no, *when* I get out, I will call Didi and tell her what happened. I will tell my friends who have become family now that Ma and Baba are gone. I know what I found out in this bathroom, I know I won't tell my now ex of this experience. He will not sympathize, nor will he believe I was trapped in the hotel bathroom. He will say I did it on purpose to get sympathy. He will say it mustn't have been that big of a deal since I got out. Or he will say it never happened, and it was all in my head. I know that, because that's what he does any time I ask him for his understanding, concern, or care. Those emotions from him are rare moments, almost never the past few years. I know I won't tell my now ex. I have to build the walls around my heart now, I know. I know.

The bathroom door bursts open, and a small young man with a handlebar moustache, wearing overalls with his name, Jose, embroidered on the bib next to the Hilton logo, rushes in, "Ma'am? You okay?"

"I'm claustrophobic," I whisper. I need a different room. I need different.

. . . .

Later, much later, I wondered how it must have been. Didi and I were back in Delhi. It was summer and the ceiling fan was still, a result of the electric company's load-shedding in the afternoon, a regular summer event. We lay on our large bed, panting in the heat like mongrel dogs, fanning ourselves with the dried palm hand fans we had brought back from Kolkata.

Since that summer, Toton-di became part of our lives, as if she had always been there. There was one grainy photo Didibhai shared once we returned back to Ma in that joint-family condominium—a blurred image of some of the married cousins with their husbands in 1960s tall hair, wives with the beehives taller than Mount Everest, in silks shining through the black-and-white image, young couples of all sizes, toothy grins, thick glasses, and there was Toton-di by herself—in the corner, her hair loose like a film star, in a sari and half-sleeve blouse, the shadow of a tree obscuring her face. I don't know what she looks like—likely like Didi, who looks like a Ghosh daughter more than me—a soft-looking movie star whose face is partially hidden.

I wondered if that brother of hers did something no brother should have. I wondered if the spaghetti straps did her in. Maybe she resisted. Maybe she didn't. Maybe she didn't feel guilt. Maybe she tried to get through life ignoring the brother who should have been a brother.

Later, when I asked Ma, she said, "Well, see, your father's family, some of them are low-life cads! Don't be like your father's family."

Which didn't help. Much, much later, I found out she hung herself in the bathroom near the steps to that house in Gariahat. I found out that she had tried to kill herself a few other times before she finally succeeded. Everyone thought she was taking a shower. She used to spend hours in that bathroom. As if she was hiding from something. From someone. Perhaps it got to be too much. Perhaps when her sari around her throat tightened, she felt better than she did about how the brother who wasn't a brother treated her. Perhaps she had no choice. Whatever it was, she decided that was it. It didn't matter that her eyes were luminous, her lips plump, and her figure stupendous. It didn't matter that she got modeling and acting job offers every day. It didn't matter that all she wanted to be was a teacher. Perhaps, one day, one moment, one minute, she said, "I can't take this anymore," and tightened the sari around her neck. Perhaps.

. . . .

We are at the FDA. The scientists demonstrate the work, and the head of the Office of In Vitro Diagnostic Device Evaluation and Safety tells us, "Good instrument. The flu epidemic is a huge threat. It can turn into a pandemic very quickly. We need a POC instrument like this in the field soon. When will you submit the final data?"[2]

At the airport, my CEO shakes my hand. "Congrats, Madhu—put this on your resume. What you demonstrated to the FDA today, it's rare. Good job."

The bathroom lockdown is a joke in our company—Madhu crawled out of the bathroom to get to the FDA, she's that dedicated! What I don't tell them is that Madhu is still in that hole, that hole she created herself. She hasn't crawled out yet. Not yet.

. . . .

I return to the place where I live with my then husband. For that weekend, I decide to make my then husband happy. I make narus like the ones Minu-di made for us that summer in 1982. Instead of jaggery, I use condensed milk. I heat the coconut flakes, add the cardamom and milk. I make the small round balls and leave them in the fridge to harden.

When I give them to my then husband, he says, "Good job, Madhu."

On average, it takes a domestic violence victim seven attempts to finally leave. Abuse isn't necessarily physical. Domestic violence can happen to anyone—young, old, strong, weak.[3] Abusive partners can be very good to and for the victim, mostly. Domestic violence has a cycle even the victim may not realize. Mine was two weeks. Two weeks of cycling between withholding interaction—even talking—and abuse, followed by two weeks of such joyous interaction that I wondered if I had imagined the previous weeks and doubted my own sanity. The two-week cycle is what I was used to, for years, so much so that it became the only thing I knew.

It took me two more years before I finally faced what I saw in that Hilton bathroom.

2 cups unsweetened coconut
flakes, ground, plus enough
to coat sweets
½ cup condensed milk

1 teaspoon ground green
cardamom seeds
2–3 saffron strands (optional)

In a nonstick pan, slowly heat the coconut on medium-low. Add the cardamom powder. When the coconut starts toasting and is fragrant, add the condensed milk and switch off the heat to prevent the mixture from burning. Stir the coconut and condensed milk quickly (it will be sticky), add the saffron if using. Place the mixture on a flat plate or pan and allow to cool.

Liberally coat your fingers with oil (I use avocado; you can use any light oil) and make small balls of the coconut–condensed milk mixture. Roll individual balls on another plate of ground dry coconut flakes and coat them liberally. Put them in mini–baking paper cups and place in the fridge until ready to serve. The narus can be frozen for three months or more, just remember to transfer them to the refrigerator overnight before serving.

Cocoa-Coconut Naru Option
Replace the cardamon and optional saffron with 3 tablespoons organic cocoa mixed in 6 tablespoons of hot water. Add cocoa-water mix to the coconut and condensed milk and prepare as instructed above.

....

CHAPTER 7

Orange, Green, and White
(An Indian Marriage)

I am not a green or an orange person. Green was a color Ma said was unlucky for her and so it automatically became so for me too. Orange was
the color of St. Clare's, the house Didi belonged to in St. Anthony's
Girls' Senior Secondary School, the rival group to my St. Joseph's, where
we sported red. Rivals didn't meet in the middle, even though Didi is my
sister, but orange was never my color. And certainly orange never mixed
with green, which, by the time I was seven was designated the unlucky
color for the entire Ghosh family. But the Indian flag was saffron, white,
and green, with a central wheel with twenty-four spokes symbolizing the
hours in a day as well as the twenty-four qualities that an uttam, or ideal
human being, should have, so it was a little inconvenient because we did
love India, just not those colors.

....

The scarf was displayed on a clothing store website from India when it
wasn't as popular to buy Indian fabrics online. The website said it was
jaypore.com. It was 2013. I was in Maryland, alone for the first time in
decades, in a house I had bought for a family that was my then husband's,
an extended family that had in all manner abandoned me.

Jaypore, I thought. Only a white person would call the city of pink, the
city of castles, the city of beautiful clothes, food, and song, Jaypore.

"It's Jaipur, stupid," I yelled at the website, alone in my house in Maryland. My voice ricocheted, reverberating off the tall ceilings in that contemporary townhouse in a planned neighborhood, close to the Metro station, movie theater, and multiple global cuisine restaurants within walking distance.

Jai. Pur. The city of victory. Jai. Pur. The city where Didi went for her honeymoon when she married my best friend from high school. I couldn't attend her wedding because Hopkins, the university where I was a postdoctoral fellow, forgot to send my travel papers to the agency on time, so I couldn't go, even though my ticket was ready and my suitcase packed.

Jaypore.com. The website was new, slick, with paisleys that attract non-Indians to spend a whole lot on a whole little. A website filled with blockprinted textiles, made by local weavers from India in pale pinks and bright blues with dazzling gold zari borders, attracting Americans wanting something exotic but not too exotic. Small blurbs popped up regularly on the screen saying, *Catherine from Utah just bought a bandhani spotted kurta.*" Or *"Maizie from New Hampshire clicked love on these tie-dye sarongs."*

Like we cared. Like anyone cared.

Well, I did that day. It was July 2013. I was on the site because if I weren't, I would be counting how many ibuprofens to swallow at one go. As of now, I had counted twenty-seven of the 800 mg ibuprofen that the ER nurse had given me for my chronic back pain.

$27 \times 800 \text{ mg} = 21,600 \text{ mg}$

21,600 mg was not for my back pain this evening. It was for the pain that was constant in my heart and my mind for months now. It was to end that pain, and I wasn't sure whether it was enough. 21,600 mg would be enough to cause liver damage, given my weight, but I wasn't sure it would kill me. I didn't know how to confirm that though. I didn't want the police to find out later from my "how to kill myself with ibuprofen" Google searches and say, "ah, she killed herself," to close the suicide case without finding out why.

Some things I know about me: I am analytical, precise, timeline-bound, scientific, and loyal. Very straightforward. I am a simple person—it's not

My wedding, March 2003

that difficult to know how my mind works. I am pretty transparent—I pride myself in that.

And right as I was doing the math, the jaypore.com flashed *here, look, scarf, green, orange, organic raw silk, $56. Ships in 2–3 days.* It was twice as much as I would pay otherwise. But it said to me: Buy me. Wrap me around you. I am yours.

I clicked on the buy button.

. . . .

My husband of eleven years, best friend of seventeen, hadn't spoken to me for nearly a year. The house that I bought with my new salary, the house I bought to fill with his family, his parents, his sister's children, his friends, the house now held me, furniture, and loneliness. I was alone. With twenty-seven tablets of 800 mg ibuprofen.

He was in America's Finest City, finishing his MBA. We had always called San Diego America's Finest City. It was our joke—that we moved from Maryland to America's Finest City and "only fine things" were possible in this coastal town that masqueraded as a city.

Ten years after I left Maryland for San Diego, I was back in Maryland again. This time, the decision wasn't dictated by the university that gave me a scholarship or the postdoctoral institution that wanted me to teach premed students. The decision was because I finally got a position in a global company that appreciated my scientific experience. I was leading a team of scientists, working in oncology diagnostics in one of the top biotech companies in the world.

March to November. Not a call. Nothing. When I tried to reach him the way I used to, the call went to voice mail. On his birthday in April, I called him multiple times. He replied by text—*I am in class at UCLA. Busy. I will call you when I am free.* He never called me back. For 214 days. When he finally called, he asked, "Have you moved on?"

As if I'm an American, to be made fun of, an American who needs to divorce so she can marry again or jump into the bed of another to forget the one before. By American, do I mean the white people who tell me how I should be? Am I American now?

These days, I sleep diagonally in my bed on a memory foam mattress. I sleep soundly without melatonin or Benadryl, after years of weeping in my pillow. Have I moved on?

. . . .

At the courthouse in 2015, the bailiff informs us that we are fifteen minutes early.

My lawyer tells me, "Trust me, I'll get him this time."

Him, like he's a squirming eel. The divorce proceedings had not been proceeding really. We keep asking him to let this finish, let's divide the assets, move on. But he wants to hold on. Multiple mediations. Phone calls. Requests for data, information. Forensics to align with assets. Let go of part of the savings. Compromise when we couldn't in our marriage. Compromise in our divorce.

He wants to negotiate when neither of us wants to be at the negotiation table. Will my lawyer get him this time? Will he let me go now? Will he understand that this has been it for so long I barely even remember the decade-long marriage, though every word he has used against me is hardwired in my brain? I have a photographic memory—I do not forget what someone said or when, or what someone wore at a particular time—I cannot wait to forget this time. Will he understand we need to let go? Just let go?

His soft-spoken Indian American lawyer taps my lawyer's shoulder, saying, "We're here too."

He's here too, in a pale blue shirt with a steel tinge, my favorite color. He knows that. His beard peppered white, another favorite. He's dressed for the occasion, our divorce. His lips smile, his eyes don't. He hugs me, like one would a friend.

I clutch my phone, my heartbeat coordinated with each vibration of incoming emails.

Surprised at my stiff hug, he says, "Kya, Madhu, is this how it is to be?"
I say, "For now, this is how it is to be."

Till we can look at each other without thinking of what it was, especially at the end of those seventeen years.

. . . .

Seven years after we met in 2003, after we moved from Maryland to America's Finest City. He in IT, I armed with my PhD and postdoctoral fellowship from Hopkins. That year, we returned to India to get married. Before I met him, my plan was to get my PhD and return to Ma and Baba. They were waiting for me to come home. I was the son Ma and Baba never had, the son who was actually the daughter but who would take care of them just like the son they yearned for would have. In Bengali, or rather, in South Asian tradition, the son is expected to take care of his parents. I was to return from my studies in America, back to Ma and Baba, and take care of them as if I were the son they had wanted when I was born.

These were unsaid rules, unsaid words, but that was the plan. And I am a planner. I wasn't to be married. I never thought I would. Then I met my now ex. Everything changed after that. All that I had promised Ma and Baba, all that I thought my life was to be, became the exact opposite. I became what my now ex wanted me to be.

In 2003, I insisted on a Bengali wedding, with our customs. This was for my parents, who needed to see their daughter was happy with her choice. The families compromised to keep everyone happy—we married in his southern Indian home, even though Bengali weddings always happen in the bride's home, with Bengali customs.

I am Bengali, an eat-fish-on-weekdays, chicken-on-weekends, literary, politics-discussing, financially unsavvy, Delhi-loving, nuclear-family-focused kind of Bengali living in America. I am a feminist Bengali. I am a scientist Bengali. He, a South Indian from Tamil Nadu, likes Tamil movies; his parents: vegetarian food, jokes, his family. Soon I grew to like those too as we made our life together.

In 2003, he and I were in our wedding finery, in Hyderabad. I, in a red Benarasi silk sari Ma and Baba brought from Kolkata, with sandal paste designs on my face. He, in a silk kurta dhoti, a gift from my parents. It was a marriage of families, a compromise, a union of two cultures, a South Indian culture allowing a Bengali culture into their strict traditions.

The first phera, or vow: we asked for nourishing food. But he raced around the fire, pulling my hand. I followed.

The seven vows, saptapadi, around the fire in a Hindu wedding are promises a man and woman make to each other. Once made, the promises are binding, forever. Fire is considered pure, signifying a new start together. Agni, the god of fire, blesses the new couple once they unite. I was not religious or traditional. But I did this for Ma and Baba. I did this for

Gluten-free chocolate cake

him and his family—I wanted him to slow down. We were to be bound forever. He raced around the fire. What else could I do but follow?

. . . .

July 2015. A year and a half after I filed for divorce in America's Finest City, I am ready for court. I wear my corporate business suit, straighten my jet-black hair, fasten my Etsy tagua nut earrings, and rearrange my jaypore orange-and-green scarf. Today, everything I wear I have bought for myself during the time he stopped talking to me. Today, I smile at my reflection. I have practiced long and hard, I pretend so well that I believe it myself.

. . . .

I met Garima Kothari in the news of her death.[1] Which is to say, I heard of her, *really* heard of her, after she was gone. It was the pandemic, and news of dying people was unfortunately and relentlessly common.

As the years in America go by, I realize I am living way more online than I had ever imagined I would. My friendships online are with strong women and allies—writers mostly. The connections are deep and strong, and yet I haven't met most of them in real life. To tell the truth, it doesn't even matter if we ever do. The connection through words is what matters.

Garima was important to this secret group of writers because she too was a writer. And a chef, a pastry chef at that. In death all the articles used the same photo of hers—large eyes, jet-black shoulder-length hair, a thick sweater—the type I'd wear when I lived on the East Coast two decades ago—leaning on a tall chair, likely in her new restaurant. She was one of us except that she got a degree in culinary arts from Le Cordon Bleu in Paris. She married someone she'd known for a while, a fellow immigrant— a "model immigrant" like herself who works hard, keeps focused, gets to work. Her husband, a financial IT Indian, is smart, a go-getter, doesn't get in trouble. Both paragons.

In February 2020, right before the pandemic brought the Great Pause, Garima reinaugurated her Indian fusion restaurant, Nukkad, "neighbor-hood corner" in colloquial Hindi.[2] She called the fare Indian "soul food," which is debatable. While the African American communities have called their food "soul food," calling Nukkad and her food the desi version may be a stretch. After all, Indian food has a spirituality, but the kind that's popular in America doesn't come from slavery or indenture. It may be soul food because it is pure and alive and possibly brightly spicy. That was her tagline, and all her social media posts had a very soft excitement combined with the almost naïve hope of an immigrant opening her own business in America, something only a few dream of achieving.

Close to the NJ-PATH train station, Nukkad was easily accessible for officegoers and commuters heading into New York City. That was the draw—location, location. If so many people were passing through this station daily, they were her customers, weren't they? With its faux-Hindi script logo on a clean blue-and-white backdrop and a sparkling counter, along with servers of Indian or South Asian descent, Nukkad was a fast-food place, with soul. It was in Jersey City, a commuter train stop away from New York City.

But in 2020, right when Garima opened Nukkad, New York City was already becoming the largest COVID-19 incubator in the country.

. . . .

2002. California pays health insurance for long-term relationships. He was on mine, even though we were unmarried, but we were as good as. He wasn't ready. We became Californians, worked hard, lived well, hiked national parks, ate tacos from Mexican dives. He played tennis—another very San Diego pastime—and much easier than surfing.

Roger Federer was his idol. He copied his moves on court, watched him on TV, standing in our tiny living room. Swishing his imaginary racquet to hit the ball on the screen.

He took tennis lessons, got his racquets restrung from the tennis couple running the small sports shack near Highway 101, played with the neighbors in the courts adjacent to our apartment.

"You should watch me sometime, Madhu," he said, his eyes twinkling.

I agreed. He liked it when I agreed with him. He linked his fingers through mine.

I sat in the stands across the tennis courts. He served twice and failed. His T-shirt stuck to his chest. Looking up, he nodded at me. I left. He didn't want me to watch him anymore.

"My life will be better if Roger wins," he said.

I laughed, "Like your life isn't good, eh?"

But he was serious. It wasn't a joke he appreciated. He stopped talking to me. This became a pattern that lasted through the marriage. It followed every Grand Slam tournament Federer played.

When the Australian Open started, he called me a bitch with an attitude. Which meant everything and nothing to me. He used words that had never been used to describe me. The first time, I fell at his feet, sorry, sorry, sorry, because the priest told us, don't go to bed angry. Our pheras, promises to the gods.

The second phera: we prayed for physical, spiritual, and mental health. He pulled me, sprinting around the fire. The priest disapprovingly shook his head saying, "Slow down, this is a promise you're making to your ancestors. Slow down."

We raced around the fire.

When Federer won, he said, "Make some tea, Madhu."

Federer walked to the podium and thanked his Australian fans. Running to the kitchen, I made his favorite Darjeeling tea. My hands shook adding honey to the cup. Roger saved my marriage that day.

. . . .

In *Salon*, an online magazine known for its readers' vicious comments to essays, Garima writes about making apple dumplings after graduating from Le Cordon Bleu—where she was taught to measure, count, ensure the fat content of each dessert—"some French-trained chefs may insist on using pistachios only from Turkey, butter with exactly 83 percent fat, fresh yeast alone for making bread, and made-from-scratch chocolate hazelnut spread that is so intense it practically instills a sense of loathing for the store-bought version."[3]

The readers' comments are missing, last I checked. Garima talks of a dessert world very different from the one I grew up in. Our desserts are thick, milk-based, voluptuous, sticky. What she has studied and makes are desserts that are delicate, measured, a science. Her essay doesn't have anyone reacting to it—almost as if her opinion isn't controversial enough for others to spend any time on.

In a Yelp review from 2020, when the restaurant is in its infancy, an irate Indian customer writes about how cold the gulab jamun was, that anybody, especially the Indian servers, should know that gulab jamun should be served warm.[4] Garima responds online in firm and politely terse sentences.

"You're asking us to fulfill an expired gift card. We heated up your dessert like you asked us to, but it wasn't enough. You told us you'd leave a negative review and now you are. We really don't know what else we can do, given that we did what we could."

I hear her frustration—albeit in a polite note—in calming irate South Asian diners who look forward to goopy cream-laden chicken dishes and thickly sweet desserts for a $9.99 buffet price in the predominantly South Asian New Jersey township. One can hear her trying to suppress her French cuisine training and swallowing her pride as she holds on to her fledging restaurant.

Did she return to her upscale high-rise apartment and tell her husband she couldn't deal with entitled desis and their tantrums? Did she hide it from him, given that investing in a restaurant near New York City must have been very expensive for them?

In India, Garima was in investment banking when she auditioned for first season of the Indian *MasterChef: India* in 2010. There's a short interview on the Cordon Bleu website about her.[5] Her appearance on the cooking show in India is a short aside in all news articles published about her. There are no videos online of her cooking. But it was that TV appearance, when she placed in the top fifteen, that prompts her to leave the world of finance for culinary arts, to head to Paris to learn how to make subtle, artistic desserts. Less than a decade later, she opens her restaurant but serves the same "Indian" food that white people were used to and that Indians demanded she provide.

Her presence appears quiet and very nonconfrontational in the food scene and online. She exists, but do we really know her as an immigrant pastry chef? As a wife? As an immigrant? Or as Garima, events planner? We don't know her.

. . . .

It is 8:45 a.m. The bailiff will call us inside soon.

My now ex asks, "How're the folks on the East Coast?"

Who, I wonder, confused. My clients? My friends in Maryland? Where I bought that townhouse and waited for him to join me for a year? My sister, the only family I have now?

"Your sister, Didi, of course!" he says, dismissively, like we were still together. Like being dismissive of me is what he can be, even now. Like the last two years didn't happen. Like he still controls me. Like he used to.

"She's fine," I say, looking into my phone.

He makes conversation. Idle chitchat. He just wants to talk. Just talk.

. . . .

The third phera: we asked for wealth. The priest said, this is serious. Not an obstacle course race.

Nearby, Didi stood near Baba, worried. Ignoring them, I followed him. It was an important promise, and much as I was doing this for the parents, I was doing it for him, my now ex.

When I started the divorce proceedings in 2014, my lawyer told me that this was a simple divorce.

But it wasn't to be. Now, over a year later, I'm still in limbo.

My lawyer talks to his, animated. He hasn't agreed to any of the proposals.

He and I stand away from our lawyers, together, apart.

"How're you, Madhu?" he asks again.

I'm fine, I nod. He clears his throat, looking ahead.

"Traveling much? Madhu?"

"Uh-huh." My iPhone glares.

"Seriously," he waves at the courthouse door, suggesting the proceedings, "after eighteen years, this is how it's gotta end, huh?"

It's my fault, it always has been. I look up. His eyes are hurt. I am the abuser. I'm the one who walked away. It must be me.

"You're stalling," I confront him. "We sent you our proposal three months ago. You replied two days before the hearing with more questions. How could you?"

"How could *I*?" he roars, "I was busy. This divorce of yours isn't my priority."

Just like our marriage wasn't a priority for you, I think.

"The ball is in your court, Madhu," he says.

"Huh?"

"My lawyer replied, didn't she?"

I feel the putrid sneakiness in that counterproposal.

The ball's in your court, Madhu.

. . . .

The fourth phera: we asked for love and respect for each other and our families. His father shook Baba's hand. Baba smiled politely, not used to people who take these rituals so lightly. His father should have pressed his hands together in a formal namaskar, but he doesn't. He shook Baba's hand as if we were Westerners.

"Slow down," I whispered.

He did. I heaved a sigh of relief.

. . . .

March was our wedding anniversary, and also the Indian Wells tennis tournament month. I made his favorites: yogurt rice with olives and grapes, rotis with potatoes and cumin, sliced cucumbers spiced with chaat masala, Laughing Cow cheese triangles, adding his beers and packaged savory Indian snacks. We drove over a hundred miles from America's Finest City to celebrate our anniversary with Roger Federer. We watched him from the nosebleed seats in the stadium. In the desert heat, Federer looked tired.

"Mononucleosis," the couple next to us said, sadly. Federer lost.[6]

We returned in silence. The silence wasn't the quiet of a couple comfortable not talking. The silence was a festering wound, of him blaming me for his favorite man's loss. My heart raced, keeping the beat with each passing second. He focused on everything else, the winding mountain road, the heat, anything but his wife next to him, asking, "Please, c'mon, what did I do now?"

....

Garima moves to the NY-NJ region around the same time my marriage falls apart. On social media, she smiles at the camera at another friend's wedding. Others comment that she looks gorgeous. Her husband, an Indian immigrant, a former Indian Institute of Technology engineering graduate—IIT, a school I graduated from, known for an admission process more difficult than Harvard's and MIT's—posts a similar happy picture from a trip they take to Europe.

His friends laugh at him trying to look cool—a stylish hat, dark glasses, casual jeans—an immigrant pose of assimilating in America as quickly as possible. He replies to that good-natured ribbing: "Shaadi ka kamaal hai," a gift of being married. He smiles at the camera, likely at his wife who took that photo. In the other selfie, she looks like a Bollywood bride—gold, stones, and a lehenga choli, her eyes still filled with hope.

The couple moves to New York, where Garima's husband completes his financial engineering graduate school from Columbia University, while Garima, who plans to start her own business, works as an event manager at New York University, catering events, lunches, dinners for dignitaries like the Clintons, tabla maestro Zakir Hussain, and Indian cooking queen Madhur Jaffrey.[7] (Her Instagram handle, @breakingbread.co, seems to be more her—light salads, dehydrated citrus wheels dipped in decadent chocolate, colorful acai bowls—international flair, with a hint or two of Indianness in an occasional samosa or rose sherbet photo. Garima's life in the late 2010s is event planning and food.

Rarely do we see her sharing her personal life. In the secret group of women writers she sometimes talks about food, what she's cooking, an article she published. She appears to be hardworking, a chef, a writer who talks about immigrant food and how difficult it is to publish. On her personal Facebook page, she writes in a few short threads that her husband isn't a social media fan. June 2019, as her birthday celebration, they head to Peru for ten days. A photo shows the two of them together, a rarity on her feed, both looking up, looking very happy—he in a fedora, she in a Patagonia jacket, holding on to each other, grinning at the camera.[8] A young couple celebrating life and learning about Peruvian cuisine. An ordinary upwardly mobile immigrant couple.

. . . .

The bailiff calls us into the courtroom. My now ex stays behind with his lawyer, who tries to convince him to let me go. "Your wife's done," she says, or so I imagine. *She's done.*

There's a custody case, then a four-year divorce proceeding before ours. The room is musty, serious. My now ex sits in the back row, two seats from me. I clutch my phone, my purse, as if holding on to them will help me hold on to the life I was now living. He closes his eyes, his left hand massaging his forehead. His face crumples, tears roll down.

He's trying hard to cry, he is, I think. I'm a bitch, I tell myself. Even his grief is contrived. Have I moved on?

. . . .

Nearly 36 percent of women and more than 27 percent of men in New Jersey have experienced some form of physical violence by an intimate partner. Three in every four domestic violence victims are women. Sixty-five percent of murder-suicides involve an intimate partner, of which 96 percent of victims are women. According to the National Coalition of Domestic Violence, the hotlines receive over 19,000 calls daily—thirteen calls every minute. Domestic violence crimes account for 20 percent of all violent crime in New Jersey.[9]

There aren't very many photos of Garima and her husband. There isn't any hint online that suggests there was violence.[10] There isn't any hint that there wasn't.

The next phera: we prayed for noble children. I told the priest, no, I'm not praying for that. Shocked, he says, it's part of the ritual.

My now ex pulled at my hand. I followed him, and he let me.

. . . .

The French Open rolled into the clay courts in May. Nadal was winning. Roger tried and failed and tried again. We weren't speaking, of course. I was accustomed to this. We were good at pretending to be a loving couple, especially to his family. His brother showed up every Saturday morning, ate my coffee cakes, watching Federer. I made strong espressos for them after their game on the cold tennis courts.

"Madhu, open a café," his brother advised, mouth filled with caramel and crispy dough.

"Yes," I laughed, "I should stop pretending to be a scientist and bake, huh?"

My now ex added, "I'll handle the money, Madhu's bad at it anyway."

Roger lost again because Nadal is the King of Clay.

"Federer has such clean lines. But that Nadal is a brute," his brother said.

"In the end, Roger owns tennis," my now ex, replied.

In the kitchen, I made my tea from Makaibari Tea Estate.[11] As a bachelor in Kolkata, Baba used to buy boxes from the tea estate directly. Ma shipped me packages when she was alive. I held those memories in my cup, with each sip of that aromatic leaf.

I don't tell him what I think of Roger or Nadal. He doesn't ask.

"Roger is king," I whispered. "But I really like Nadal's spirit," I said to the softly warm tea.

His family didn't notice that he hadn't spoken with me all summer. Not his brother, his cousins, their spouses, or his parents. Then, during Wimbledon, he started talking to me again. His family still didn't notice.

. . . .

By the time I headed to a therapist, riddled with Catholic-school guilt that I was responsible for my now ex's anger, silence, and disappointment, I was unsure of who I was. I tried to be the model immigrant, the model wife, the model scientist, the model feminist. I had failed in all of them.

I told the young therapist with a neatly trimmed goatee, "My in-laws have been very nice to me always, throughout the seventeen years I've known them."

And he replied quietly, "Have they? Why do you keep defending them even when their son treats you like this? Do they stand up for you when he does?"

I had no answers. I hear the words, "narcissistic personality disorder," "borderline," and "emotional abuse," and I couldn't connect with them or attribute that to my now ex.[12]

I insisted to my therapist, "I'm a feminist. I am strong."

He nodded, his brown eyes kind. "Sure. Who says strong women can't be abused? Emotional abuse is silent. That's why this is difficult for you."

. . . .

The sixth phera: we asked for a peaceful long life with each other.

"Madhu, it's late, the reception will be delayed, c'mon!"

I was silent, I wished him a peaceful life. I followed.

. . . .

The proximity to NYC, which was a good thing for a restaurant, is exactly the reason Nukkad needed to shut down in March. The COVID-19 infection spreads through the city like an uncontrolled fire.[13] No one knows what works with the disease—are young people safe, are children? Are the elderly, immune-compromised the only ones at risk? How about the mutations in the virus? After diagnosis, what will help? Steroids or non-anti-inflammatories? How many ventilators do we have? Every day, things change. Businesses have to shut down during the Great Pause. We don't know how long we need to stay home. Nukkad closes its doors and Garima focuses on a plan to keep the business alive. She is, at that time, three months pregnant.

. . . .

Our lawyers beckon us, we head to the same part of the courthouse, separated in two groups, a few feet apart.

. . . .

My lawyer says, "Well, there will be mediation, Madhu, you can't avoid that."

"We failed it last time, and I'm not paying again."

My voice is strong, my eyes dry. I won't collapse again. Not in front of him.

"Trust me," my lawyer says, her blue eyes piercing mine, "I'll make him comply."

We all come together, huddling like we're on a football field.

My lawyer tells him, "You need to promise we'll compromise, so you can move on. Promise?"

He nods dismissively, as if that's a ridiculous question to ask. "Of course," he says, "let's discuss the things we agree on now. We can take on the big-ticket items at mediation."

He says it as if he knows how to compromise. I look down. I don't engage. My lawyer says, "How can we negotiate when we don't agree on anything?" I whisper to my lawyer.

"We can only try, " she says, unconvincingly.

. . . .

Wimbledon was fierce. Roger needed to win, and Nadal was a phoenix rising after each fall. Roger said he was well, but here too he lost. He cried at the awards ceremony, and Nadal hugged him the way my now ex's brother hugged him that Saturday. Silent, my now ex headed to the bedroom and closed the door.

I hoped he would speak to me before Labor Day, the US Open. If Roger wins, this marriage is saved.

In 2008, the US Open was hot and muggy. My now ex headed to Flushing Meadows to watch Federer. I noted that he didn't ask me to join him. But he called me daily on his train ride from his friend's place in New Jersey to the tennis tournament. He was in good spirits, and so I was too.

"He's very strong, he'll do it this time."

I agreed, even though I liked Nadal more. Roger played against Andy Murray, the Scotsman that year. He won, 6–2, 7–5, 6–2.[14] Even I was excited. Roger was family now; he had to win to keep us together. For that year, the marriage was saved. He spoke to me when he returned.

. . . .

Around the end of April, Mayukh Sen interviews Garima in a quick nine-minute phone call to ask how the pandemic was affecting her business as an immigrant, as a "fusion" Indian chef, as the owner of a business that exists not in the heart of New York City, but in Jersey City.[15] In a *Vox* article, Sen doesn't name Garima but notes, "the pandemic could wipe out eateries that showcase immigrant fare. Some owners fear facing prejudices that their cuisines aren't profitable enough to save because they aren't continental European."[16] Later, he writes to say this is what he had talked to her about—that the grants were going to the restaurants serving pizza and Italian food, not desi soul cuisine.[17]

Business stops within a few weeks of Nukkad's opening. PATH commuters stay home. New York events, city crowds, everything stalls—everyone stays home.

Garima applies for small-business loans, grants, and then starts a food delivery program while she waits, like all of us in the Great Pause.

. . . .

March 2013. The last day my now ex and I spoke before he fell silent for 214 days, I called him from Maryland. He was completing his MBA, which was low-residency, meaning he could take the courses online and meet on-site every other weekend.

My job led me to travel all over the world most of each month. We bought a townhome so his parents could stay with us. I used my savings to make the down payment. But he didn't move in with me. Boxes still strewn in the new home, I worked eighteen-hour days and waited for him to join me. Until then, I saved the marriage by heading to San Diego every month. No one at work knew what I did at home to keep my family intact. No one.

I pleaded with him to come to Maryland. Help me unpack.

He said, no, my MBA. "I have to be in UCLA. I'm busy."

Yes, but only on two weekends each month. "Come," I pleaded, "We bought a new home. Help me unpack."

He said, "I'll stay in San Diego. You take care of my parents."

"Sure, but if they come, won't you be with me too? You're in between jobs, so—"

But he said no, my MBA. My classes. And tennis. And my brother.

For the first time in our lives together, I said, "If your parents stay with me, you do too."

"No. In fact, I'll never come to Maryland."

"Why?"

"I'll never come to a house where my parents aren't welcome," he said.

"No, no," I protested. "That's not what I said. My parents are dead, your parents are mine. Why wouldn't I want your parents here? They have a unit all to themselves, they don't have to climb steps."

"No."

"I didn't say they weren't welcome," I pleaded. "Please help me."

He hung up. I called him. Many times. As I always have. He didn't pick up. On his birthday in April, three weeks after he stopped taking my calls, I called him multiple times. He didn't pick up. I left him messages. And, finally, I texted him, *I am heading to Germany on work. It would be great if you could call.* When I landed in Dusseldorf and switched on my phone, his note said, *I am in class. I cannot call. I will when I am free.*

He didn't call me for 214 days.

. . . .

Nukkad's launch is in February 2020. While her husband is listed as co-owner, she's the face of Nukkad. A few months earlier, she notes on @breakingbread.co on Instagram, where she posted only food photos—that she'd tried to get a food license to sell samosas and Indian street food at a neighborhood farmer's market, but the officials said samosas are like empanadas. The farmer's market decision makers already had a vendor selling a form of "samosas," so didn't need another one to compete with the empanada business, even though samosas are South Asian, empanadas are well, not.

Even in her disappointment, Garima seems resigned, unwilling to call this a racist and ignorant decision. Her followers react with shock and outrage. Garima doesn't push this—her next post is another pretty food picture, delightfully styled, softly backlit to highlight the dish, as if she'd rather focus on what she is proud of, what she can control. A few months later, in February 2020, she opens Nukkad. A far cry from French cuisine or even her catering business of familiar "Western" amuse-bouche small plates, Nukkad offers safe menu items with standard South Indian fare, such as idlis, dosas, and masala chai along with North Indian chaat. Although very similar to other Indian restaurants, the difference in Nukkad is that Garima wants to create a place for adda, a Bengali word for a neighborhood gathering to gossip, chat, be part of the community. Her social media says she grew up in Kolkata, and her love for Marwari and Bengali cuisine is all over the regional foods she showcases online. Even though she may be non-Bengali, her highlighting Nukkad as a place for adda meant we glimpsed Kolkata in her vision.

That was in February 2020. The first COVID-19 case was less than a month away in New York City, one train stop away from Jersey City. Ironically, it is location, location, location that did the neighborhood restaurant in. By the end of March, the lockdown forced Nukkad to close, less than two months after its grand opening.

. . . .

The seventh phera: we asked for companionship, togetherness, loyalty, and understanding as a team. The priest held his hands and asked my now ex to fold them in front of the fire, "Sir, she is now your ard-hangini, your wife. What you do from now on, she's an equal part of it. There's no shame, no ego between you two. Never go to bed angry. Even if you're in the right, make sure you resolve all agreements with your ardhangini before you go to sleep. You're now married in front of the holy fire, congratulations."

They call our names at the courthouse. I get up. My lawyer stands to the left in front of the judge, his to the right. I hold the swinging half door open for him. As I always have. He enters and stands next to his lawyer.

. . . .

For two hundred days, I waited for him to call. To tell me this was a silly misunderstanding. That he's sorry. That his parents would move in and that he would come with them. That he'd help me unpack. That we would start afresh. That he'll talk again to me. That he'll see how I'm losing myself so I didn't lose him.

When the Grand Slams started, I flipped the channels, to E!, cooking competitions, anything that wasn't tennis. So I could still breathe and continue breathing while I waited. Waited for his call that said, "Yes, I'm sorry I thought of me before us."

For two hundred days, I lived so I could last through the day and the next and the next. Then he called.

"So, have you moved on?"

"What does that mean," I wondered.

That's what Americans ask, don't they? Are we that American? He wanted this to end. His voice didn't shake. I didn't let my wails escape me either.

The next day, he sent me an email: *how about this online divorce group? It'll be quick.*

I didn't reply. What was the point? I packed his things. Music, photos, the wedding shirt my parents gave him. His parents' medicines, clothes, CDs. The brass gods and goddesses placed neatly on a shelf in their bed-room. His tennis shoes, ties he never used, shoes he never wore. Roger

Federer's red cap that I gave him on his fortieth, four years ago. I labeled each box FRAGILE and TOP, an arrow pointing where the top was, using his name for the movers to differentiate his boxes from mine. I was moving back to San Diego, to a new job, the first time alone in every way, with my own boxes, and my own new life without him.

. . . .

2015. My lawyer addresses the judge. I look ahead. I don't know whether my now ex's eyes are still filled with tears. The man I loved is still the man I love. Only, that man doesn't exist. The ball is in your court.

. . . .

On April 26, 2020, around 7:15 a.m., the police find Garima's body in her luxury high-rise apartment near Nukkad. There are brutal injuries to her upper torso, and her death is ruled a homicide. They don't say whether she was beaten, sliced, shot, or all of the above. It doesn't matter.

Forty minutes later, her husband's body is found floating between Montgomery Street and Exchange Place in the Hudson River. Garima was thirty-five; her husband, two years older. Their deaths are noted: murder-suicide. YouTube videos from India swirl online within hours—the NRI couple who owned a restaurant (they make sure to note that Nukkad was a jointly owned venture—after all, a woman can't own her own business, can she?), and how COVID and the financial burden had forced her husband to kill the chef. Garima is five months pregnant at the time of her death.

. . . .

It is 2016. Mediation has failed three times. He has stalked me, waiting near my car at my office parking lot. He has argued loudly with me there, my office colleagues walking by, curious, but respecting my privacy. After not talking to me for a year, he has called to call me names. Asked me to give details of the jewelry my parents gave me as a wedding gift, staking claim to it for the division of assets—Ma and Baba's gift, to be divided between us because that was the only control he now has. Asked for alimony because now my career is on an upward swing—that's what he tells the mediators. Upward swing.

Today, we are in front of the judge. I think we will be ending this. He doesn't want to give me 50 percent of the assets in accordance with California divorce laws. I have a zero-bank balance because I used up my savings for the marriage and then on this divorce. He's telling the judge that he is still working on his MBA and has no earning power. My lawyer is rebutting that—after all, he's been working in IT in global companies for over two decades and already has a master's degree and now is getting his MBA. He has earning power and potential, my lawyer says. He again asks for alimony. He's asking for my paycheck.

I wrap my green-and-orange jaypore scarf around my neck. My hair is straight, loose, long—I never used to wear it this way—he didn't like it loose, open, like that. He said it meant I was trying too hard to look attractive. My skirt is a professional one, my jacket is dark. My scarf is bright and tells me I am not afraid anymore.

. . . .

On April 19, 2020, Garima announces to her Facebook community that Nukkad is open for DIY dosa kits, food-to-go orders. "I would so appreciate the support of the community at this point of time!" she notes in quiet desperation.

In his *Eater* article, "Who Gets an Obituary?," Sen notes: "Coverage of Kothari was so scant in her lifetime that some may reason that she wasn't yet 'famous' enough, that her restaurant was too young, to justify immediate reporting on her death. This argument is precisely the issue at hand, one that exposes the inherent bias of a food media whose narrative gaze skews towards white, materially advantaged, cis male chefs, who also tend to have aggressive public relations teams that help to guarantee media saturation."[18]

The pandemic and the overall focus on dramatic stories, restaurant closures, and the raging infection leaves domestic violence victims like Garima as a footnote. She was also an aspiring chef who could have made her take on Indian cuisine relatable in America. But she was murdered, and she is now a statistic that may not be connected to deaths from COVID-19. She may be considered a domestic violence statistic. Such violence in South Asian communities is shielded from "white American" attention—it doesn't warrant *that* kind of attention, especially to us model immigrants, does it?

. . . .

Many immigrants from South Asia come here to fill a particular role that this country gives us. A doctor. An engineer. A scientist. A banker. We try to be what America wants us to be. To be something other than that means a break away from labels, from our motherland as well as our adopted country. Garima left investment banking to become a chef. She was only getting started.

Sometimes violence of the type that took her life is a result of emotional turmoil. Sometimes it's a "crime of passion." Sometimes such violence is a culmination of multiple smaller egregious acts that no one else heard about because they were "disagreements" between married partners.

After all, for immigrants, financial stability is what we crave, given that it's what we moved to America for. If that sliver of equilibrium is pulled from under us, what are we to do? What is a man to do when the fusion restaurant he owns with his wife is going under along with his life savings? What is his wife, who gave up her professional career in finance to dive into another one that she's passionate about, to do? What's a man to do when he feels that by killing his pregnant wife he can control his world, which is spinning out of control? What's a man to do when he leaves his dying wife with stab wounds to her upper torso but go to the Hudson River? What's he to do except jump, knowing he will drown, and the subtle lights from the city that enticed him and his nearly dead wife blink alluringly from the other side of the water?

. . . .

It's been many years since that day in court. Almost as many since I saw him in person. It's been as many years since I have been that woman at the courthouse—even though I still have that scarf and even though I mostly wear my hair down. I am still that woman, but mostly I am not.

Sometimes I wonder what attracts me to stories of strangers, of strong women who knowingly get into abusive relationships—or do they? Why do I devour news articles about women who make immensely rational, smart decisions all the time, and then suddenly, without much logic, fall in love with someone who pulls them down? According to Shannon Thomas, author of *Healing from Hidden Abuse*, success and strength in such women attract abusive narcissists and psychopaths.[19] These women, besides being strong, are also extremely empathic people.

We may never know what happened to make Garima's husband attack her. We may never know the trigger. We may never know how many times before this had she been attacked. Sometimes, I too don't know whether I imagined what happened to me, Baba's daughter, that I let my then husband treat me the way he did. I also don't know why, for years and years, I held on to him, thinking that without him, I'd be nothing. I only know that's what it was and how it's been years after I was that woman. But sometimes, more rarely now, but sometimes, I do wonder why.

....

Today I measure out six tablespoons of organic cocoa, add it to one cup of gluten-free almond flour, a pinch of salt, a half cup of date sugar, and half a teaspoon of baking soda. Adding one cup of oil with half a cup of water and three eggs, I mix the batter with a spatula, even though I could use a blender, because I like the feel of the graininess of the flour as I scrape the bowl. I add a few drops of olive oil to the pan to coat it, then dust it with more gluten-free flour. I bake the chocolate olive oil cake at 325 degrees Fahrenheit for an hour. I glaze it with three tablespoons of cacao mixed with two tablespoons of olive oil and a quarter cup of sugar. It isn't the coffee cake I baked a decade ago. It isn't a dessert I gave my now ex and then husband, hoping he would like it, hoping he will be kind to me after. No.

This gluten-free chocolate olive oil cake is better, so much better. I cut myself a generous slice.

I grew up Indian, knowing divorce wasn't an option, and here we are. I joke with my friends—everything I feared would happen, happened. Parents died. Husband left me. Don't have a family. I'll die alone. Didn't think I'd be living in America. Didn't think I'd live so far from India. But here we are. Here we are. Sometimes, when the biggest fears come true, we have no choice but to carry on—and carry on well.

I take a bite of the still warm cake, a modified version of Nigella Lawson's recipe.[20]

"Not bad," I tell the dog, who looks up at me in anticipation. I shake my head at her and she settles down with a complaining groan.

CHAPTER 8
....

Of Papers, Pekoe, Poetry, and Protests in 2019 India

The homesickness Ma and Baba felt when they left Kolkata for Orissa and then Delhi manifested itself in many things, but mostly tea. Apparently, the North Indians didn't know how to make or select tea, only Bengalis did. Or so they said.

Every summer we received three large tin boxes in the very intermittent and quite irregular Indian mail. Wrapped in burlap with distinct railway letters, multiple stamps glued on haphazardly, and jute string sewed through to seal the metal boxes in the gunny sack. For good measure, each side of the box was sealed with red wax, or lac, as we called it in India, and shipped from North Bengal. Sometimes we'd get all the tins, sometimes just one. Any time we received all three was a joyous day in the Ghosh household. The tea estate, Makaibari, was a publicly traded company and the only one that Baba owned stocks and/or bonds in, or so he said.[1] This was Baba's seal of approval, investing in a company that brought him joy.

What I do know now is that it was the only Bengali-owned tea estate. Surprisingly, the British, who had everything to do with tea in India, didn't have any links with this estate. This in itself was a feat, given that most Darjeeling tea estates produce tea for the West, in particular, for British tea companies. Recently, I checked to see the ticker symbol for Makaibari, but I couldn't find it. Was it then not a publicly traded company—a story I had heard all through my childhood? Regardless, from the seventies to well in the nineties, Baba and Ma eagerly awaited the first flush—the small bud with the first leaf from the tea plant—to arrive on an abysmally slow-moving goods train to our Bengali neighborhood in New Delhi.

Makaibari, which literally translates as "home of cornfields," is a fourth-generation Bengali tea estate. They call their workers partners and allow them to host tourists in their homes to supplement their income as tea plantation employees. If one can pay one's workers well, they wouldn't need to share their homes with tourists, would they? Another way to look at this would be that the tea estate empowers women to find other entrepreneurial means of income and gives them the opportunity and ability to do so. Bed-and-breakfast outfits are one of those opportunities.

They also have USDA-approved organic teas that can now be purchased online globally. It is indeed a modern estate with modern ways of doing business, a uniquely Indian gift to others.

"Oder cha ta is the very best," Baba always proclaimed when the boxes came and then proceeded to repeat the story of the Makaibari shares and bonds he had bought, as had his mother, a story that had no value or meaning for his daughters.

. . . .

Those days, we had bone china cups for daily use. We kept a separate thicker (and therefore cheaper) cup and saucer for the maid who came to clean the house every day.

No matter how egalitarian and progressive the family, there was and continues to be a distinct difference between upper-middle-class families and their help. Feudalism in current day India continues to exist in subtle and interesting ways. The "invisible class," the help, enables a robust contemporary Indian economy, enables the gentrified to have a level of unprecedented luxury, and yet, as the term suggests, they are unseen. That, however, is a separate discussion.

What we had in Chittaranjan Park, the neighborhood formerly known as East Pakistan Displaced Persons Colony, were bone china everyday use sets, a few thicker cups for the help—the driver, the gardener, the maid.

Masala chai

For guests, we had a separate set of even finer bone china with gold painted rims and wispy blue flower patterns all along the edge and on the bottom of each small curvy cup. As a child, I used to think the crockery was made of dead Chinese people, and yet I apparently didn't feel any remorse drinking from cups made of bones. That logic still doesn't make sense.

Ma would steep two or three teaspoons of that expensive tea in hot water, pouring the pale golden-brown liquid into the white cups, adding a dash of full-fat milk with a teaspoon of sugar crystals. It was a daily ritual. As Bengalis, we were used to sweetening everything, a teaspoon or two of sugar in a tiny cup was an everyday occurrence. We had tea five or six times a day. Wash cups, rinse in hot water, add tea, milk, sugar. Dip a Nice biscuit with sugar crystals on top in it, sip the tea slowly. Clean the cups again in hot water with Vim cleaning powder and let dry. Repeat.

These days, I only drink coffee. The best medium-roast blends, but coffee nonetheless. I haven't added sugar to my coffee in decades—I feel it only dilutes the flavor. I still add a splash of milk because the casein protein in milk reduces the caffeine acidity, making the coffee a packed-with-flavor wake-me-up.

My childhood was Baba calling out to Ma, "Shono, aar ek cup cha banaabe?" Listen, could you make me another cup of tea?

I never heard Ma say no.

Those three tins lasted the entire year, and again, like clockwork, three more showed up the next summer.

Cha and the act of making cha was an act of love, an act of family.

. . . .

On December 4, 2019, ordinary students, citizens, and the people of Assam, Delhi, Meghalaya, Arunachal Pradesh, and Tripura are on the streets, protesting against the Citizenship Amendment Act (CAA).[2] The bill is enacted into law a week later. The act is expected to fast-track citizenship for non-Muslim immigrants and refugees from Bangladesh, Pakistan, and Afghanistan. The operative term is non-Muslim. This act is a direct government-sanctioned discriminatory diktat with the aim of excluding Muslims. With the CAA comes the need for documentation to prove one's refugee status, one's name, and one's religion, along with one's place of birth.

Given that many refugees of all religions arrive in India facing persecution in their home country, documentation is light at best. Migrants arriving from neighboring countries, people born in villages before a certain year, displaced, nomadic refugees, and the illiterate will have no access to the required documentation. In addition to the CAA, there is also the Nationwide Register of Citizens (NRC). The registry, besides being alarmingly discriminatory against Muslims, the largest minority in secular India, is also discriminatory against women who change their names after marriage, have different iterations of their names (in English versus their mother tongue), and people who have multiple iterations of their names. A Sheila may be Sheela, Shailah, or, like my mother's name, Sila. Most documentation could be rejected on the basis of a spelling mismatch, name change, or adoption of one's husband's surname.

In India, as of 2021, the census data indicates that the literacy rate is about 75 percent, with women's rate at about 65 percent. Additionally, this indicates that at least a quarter of Indians, aged seven and above are illiterate, of which about a third are women.[3] Women have the most to lose in contemporary India under this nationalist government. For those outside of India, primarily in America, all this was hidden under impeachment crises, blustering Presidential denials, proud red hats, and volatile conversations during the holiday season in December 2019.

I follow the CAA protests online, the only place I'm in that still keeps me connected to my native country. Indian websites, even the questionable nationalistic ones, emphasize that ordinary citizens are fed up and done with their version of Trump. At the same time, the *New Yorker* presents an essay by Dexter Filkins on Narendra Modi, the nationalistic prime minister of India. It is one of the very few Western essays that highlight alarming parallels between Modi and the forty-fifth president of the United States.[4]

The CAA soon becomes a hashtag, #CAAProtests. The amendment changes how India will process citizenship applications from refugees who arrived before 2015. The amendment benefits religious groups from Afghanistan, Pakistan, and Bangladesh, except Muslims, Rohingyas from Myanmar, Buddhist refugees from Tibet, and Tamil refugees from Sri Lanka.

. . . .

When I went back to Chittaranjan Park after both my parents' deaths and the end of my marriage, Makaibari tea was readily available in the local sundries store. It was the most expensive tea our family had known and, hands down, was a class apart from the buraada, tea that has the texture of gunpowder, with a deep brown color and little to no flavor. The generic varieties from the Lipton, BRÜ, or the PG Tips were no match to Makaibari. To see those foil-sealed packages available so readily in Delhi grocery stores brought me such delight. Five years back, I brought back two packets, vacuum-sealed, to San Diego. I haven't had the heart to open them yet. I hoard them like gold at a desi wedding.

....

To say tea was used as a colonizing weapon would be an understatement. Indians did not drink tea till the mid-nineteenth century. For centuries, tea, or cha, was China's. Green tea was the beverage of choice. The British royal courts were introduced to this unfamiliar drink from China by Catherine of Braganza, the Portuguese queen consort of Charles II in the seventeenth century. Still considered exotic and foreign, tea took its time becoming the British people's choice of drink. In 1664, the East India Company placed its first order of a hundred pounds of tea from China to Britain.[5] By 1750, the company had imported over four million pounds of tea, making it the most profitable trading good from the "Far East," and it made sure to hold the trading monopoly on behalf of the Crown for centuries. By 1784, the import tax was slashed by Prime Minister William Pitt the Younger, making tea part of the British commoners' lives. The reason for the tax reduction was that smuggling had led to a glut of tea within the company coffers. The company then decided that it now needed to be sold not only to British commoners but to other colonies.

The East India Company set its sights on America to offload tea along with capturing profit through exorbitant taxes. The Boston Tea Party in 1773 was an active American revolt, in which patriots threw 342 chests of tea from British ships into the Boston Harbor water.[6] The American patriots refused to pay the tariff on tea, in effect creating a stalemate between the Crown and the colonies in a battle cry sparking the American War of

Independence. Boston led the charge. Similar revolts happened in New York, Philadelphia, and Charleston.

In India, by 1834, the Crown had colonized disparate kingdoms and inserted itself in kingdom and provincial politics for decades. The East India Company took over trade, land, and through political liaisons managed to rule on behalf of the Crown, using British and its own policing armies to transform itself from a trading company to a ruling power. After the Revolt of 1857, the Indian subcontinent was handed over to the Crown as a colony. British rule continued until 1947, when India gained its independence.

After 1834, this maneuvering meant that British control over China became tenuous. Tea costs went up, trade was vastly imbalanced, and the company now looked to grow tea elsewhere. Appointed by Governor-General Lord William Bentinck in 1834, the Tea Committee recommended that tea seeds from China be transported to Indian mountainous regions—in particular, Assam, where the local tea plants were already being harvested, and other areas similar to Assam in climate and forest areas, such as Darjeeling and Siliguri in northern Bengal.[7] Four years later, twelve chests of Assam tea arrived in the London offices for auction. Two decades later, Indian plantations were cultivating about half a million pounds of Assam tea for consumption in the West. By the mid-nineteenth-century, tea was available to Indians. The most commonly available tea was black, grown in Indian tea plantations. This tea couldn't be as easily adulterated as green (with sheep dung or adulterants such as other parts of the plant) and was considered the best option to be cultivated and sold in India.

To make tea attractive to a people accustomed for centuries to sticky sugary-sweet drinks such as lassi, sherbets, or savory yogurt ghol (or chaas), the British had to make this beverage attractive. Indians had transformed cane sugar into an art by the first century CE through North Indian sugarcane farming.[8] Most common in use within Indian households, however, was the unfiltered, unrefined sugar component from date or other palm trees, also called gur or jaggery.[9] To reduce the harshness of black tea, a

Chai in clay cup

splash of milk; to enhance the taste, spices such as cloves, cinnamon, and ginger; to make it desi or native tea, sugar crystals. Thus, India converted Chinese green tea to Indian "masala chai" a century and a half ago.[10] Once Indians were hooked, the East India Company and the Crown colonized India not only in spirit but gastronomically.

Gorkha and Indian workers managed Assam and Darjeeling tea plantations as estate staff. The workers are considered independent and continue to live on the property with their families. Estate employees are given free lodging and a set of clothes annually. For all practical purposes, this continues to be an indentured group of people. The "estates"—the term used for these plantations in contemporary India—could very well have been cultivating cotton in the American South.

Since the indentured workers at least have the freedom to leave the tea estates or, if they continued to work there, to live in their assigned quarters with their family members, one could argue that it isn't imprisonment or slavery as it was in the American Deep South. However, with little to no financial means, without education or life skills to survive outside the estates, and because trained in only tea plantation work, Indian indentured workers are completely dependent on the system that indentures them. Even if they may not be slaves, the world of indentured tea workers is a Catch-22 situation. They are now colonized by their own.

. . . .

There are many reasons for protest in 2019 India. The Assam/Arunachal Pradesh protests are about reduced opportunities for citizens, especially because of migrants and refugees. The question remains how the government can determine how best to manage the migrant population without actively excluding Muslims. For Delhi, Kolkata, and the state of Uttar Pradesh, the protests are complicated by citizenship rules. The exclusion of Muslim refugees from the citizenship process indicates that the nationalistic and pro-Hindu government in particular under Modi's leadership is actively making India—currently predominantly Hindu—into an unabashed nationalistic Hindu country.[11]

. . . .

In India, as it is in America and elsewhere, students, activists, and citizens lead protests. Others riot. In New Delhi, two politically active, socialist-leaning, freethinking schools, Jawaharlal Nehru University and Jamia Millia Islamia, led the charge. Both schools became battlefields. Rioters joined student rallies, burning public buses and property and attacking students. WhatsApp, Facebook Live, and Twitter enabled communication and miscommunication—and India, a country with more than 65 percent of its citizens under the age of thirty-five, saw the effect of social media in real time.[12]

Reminiscent of anti-Vietnam war protests, the placards and signs that students carried articulated their rage.

. . . .

Growing up in New Delhi, going to a Catholic school with classmates from different states and multiple religions was considered a bonus. Last names such as Anthony (my closest friend) and Latif (the next closest, with whom I am still connected on social media) weren't an anomaly. We sampled different foods from different cultures every time a classmate invited us home. Learning their religious customs, foods, and rituals was par for the course. Never were there culturally insulting comments that needed correction. I am likely romanticizing this, because we Indians as a country are very racist—colorism is our middle name,[13] and frankly, having a Christian or a Muslim friend as a six- or eight-year-old is considered cute. Marrying one is a different matter.

Since 2009, conspiracy theories propagated by the nationalist Hindu groups associated with the current ruling party claimed Muslim men were actively coercing and kidnapping—and marrying—Hindu women as part of a "love jihad." This stereotyping of Muslim men fed the nationalistic Hindu government claim of a global Islamist conspiracy to lure and corrupt Hindu women.[14] Love jihad has its roots in Partition, when the violence, besides the murder of Hindu and Muslim men, was systematically targeted against women from both religions. Rape, kidnapping, and murder, as well as forced conversion of women to the other religion, along with the trauma and societal shame of the resulting "dishonor," was a convenient means of suppression. While love jihad may be a conspiracy theory, the British nevertheless divided India on the basis of religion and by encouraging religious strife, which in current-day India has morphed into nationalistic pride and, in turn, hatred for the "other," despite the country's being secular by law.

But India, a conglomerate of kingdoms and cultures, has been a country of many religions for centuries—we've learned to live with each other and, as they say in corporate-speak, to "swim in our swim lanes." There is a tenuous religious peace and cultural and regional freedom. We grew up on a razor's edge and balanced ourselves so as not to veer into any uncomfortable discussions or actions that might destroy long-term friendships and relationships.

Independent India—which exists because the British divided India from East Bengal and West Pakistan, regardless of how little the culture, food, and customs of the two regions had in common (the only binding factor being that both regions had predominantly Muslim populations)—is built on aggrieved egos, politics, machinations, and yes, relationships. The waxing and waning of love for Pakistan and Pakistani film actors, ghazal and qawwali singers,[15] followed by skirmishes and wars at the Indo-Pak borders and mountains that have yielded many a patriotic song and movies featuring brawny men with desh bhakti—or devotion to their country—is so normal that it doesn't even make it to international news forums.

What has happened in the three decades I've been out of my country is that the Hindu nationalism skulking furtively in the background is now in focus and center stage, audacious, fearless, and ever-present—a chest-thumping declaration of rude and brash achievement.

. . . .

Lately, I realize I am turning into the "old desi aunty" I was afraid of becoming—I reminisce about the good old days of student protests, when the ideals were pure, the cause was universal, and the need was urgent. Was it really so pure? Was it really successful? Were student protests enough to hold the government accountable?

The Naxalite movement fighting for native indigenous tribe groups and their land rights started in Naxalbari in 1967 Bengal as a peasant uprising against the government, with strong support from students and activists.[16]

In present-day India, the movement has gained momentum, along with Maoists fighting to establish a "people's government" by overthrowing the current democratically elected government and working for the indigenous peoples and their land rights. In the interior Chhattisgarh regions, despite heavy Indian army military action, the insurgent attacks have been successful.[17]

The Citizenship Amendment Act protests have brought us back to Naxalite days, although they are not as violent as the Maoist killings.[18] In 2019, the CAA protests started in the northeastern part of India and overtook the capital. Protesters use poetry as a weapon. Any violence is perpetrated on the protestors—by the police or fringe nationalistic groups.

. . . .

By December 12, 2019, twenty-seven protestors, mostly Muslim, had died in police clashes. The internet is shut down, university hostels are targeted, while students from Muslim universities, such as Aligarh and Jamia Milia, are beaten by the police, arrested, or both. Sadaf Jafar, a Lucknow journalist is on Facebook Live when she is attacked, handcuffed, and arrested.[19] Images of students walking out of their university campuses with their hands up like criminals are paraded daily in most Indian media. The Human Rights Watch asks the Indian government to cease unnecessary force on demonstrators—a mild warning—given that the situation is as horrifying as the ongoing Hong Kong protests.[20]

. . . .

Of course, poetry and protests are best friends. Writer and comedian Varun Grover penned the rallying cry for the CAA protests titled "Hum kagaz nahi dikhayenge" (We will not show our papers, or The NRC papers we will not show).[21] The "papers" in question are the National Registry of Citizens papers, which must be produced on demand as proof of citizenship. Grover's poem has become a rallying cry for India. In English translation, the first four stanzas of the poem are as follows:

The (NRC) papers, we will not show
Dictators will come and go
The papers we will not show
Dictators will come and go
The papers we will not show

You blind us with tear gas
You poison our waters
That our love will sweeten
And we'll drink it all in one go
The NRC papers, we will not show
The NRC papers, we will not show

This nation is all we got
Where Ram Prasad is also "Bismil"
How will you divide the motherland
That has blood and sacrifice of every Indian

Raise your batons all you can
Shut down every train you can
We will walk, we will flow
The NRC papers, we will not show[22]

According to Grover, the protest in 2019 is "almost like a cry for help by people who have no other power." The impact of this poem on the NRC protests was similar to the October 2016 call on Facebook urging supporters of the Water Protectors to "check in" to Standing Rock Reservation. In April 2016, more than ninety Native American nations converged on Standing Rock Reservation in North Dakota to protest against the construction of the Dakota Access Pipeline because it would threaten sacred tribal sites and dangerously affect the tribe's water supply. By October, it was alleged that Morton County sheriff's department was tracking and surveilling the activists at the protest camp, using Facebook's location check-in feature. After the viral call to check in was posted to "overwhelm and confuse" the authorities, more than a million people, including me, checked in, hoping to reduce official surveillance of the tribal activists. Grover's protest poem was a similar call to action in solidarity with the people who were forced to show the NRC papers to prove their citizenship and, in turn, their allegiance to India.[23]

. . . .

In 2016, after almost seven years away, I return to New Delhi, a city I cannot recognize. Flyovers, glass-and-concrete modern buildings touching the sky, the sky a polluted Beijing-gray, and people wearing antipollution masks as if we were living in a not-quite-futuristic movie, spending money in multistory malls as a means of passing time.

This is four years before the pandemic, and wearing a mask is as alien as this polluted air. Spending money while the poor get poorer is pretty familiar because I live in America. But I don't fit in. People are more capitalistic in India than where I now live, it appears. Everyone has at least a couple of cars, a couple of phones, and too much cash in their pockets.

I misspeak. By the people, I mean the middle and upper middle class. The divide between the poor and middle class in India has grown exponentially. In fact, there isn't a middle class really—it's a clear distinction between the rich and the poor. So what do people do when they have no other power? Poetry has a power, much as the poor, once unleashed, are relentless.

. . . .

Bear with me—we Indians are storytellers. So let me tell you a story. It is February 13, 1986. Pakistani singer Iqbal Bano, in a black sari, heads to the stage at the Alhamra Arts Center in Lahore.[24] The country is under the dictatorship of General Zia ul-Haq, who in a military coup had deposed Prime Minister Zulfikar Ali Bhutto in 1977. Bhutto had appointed poet Faiz Ahmed Faiz, considered one of the foremost Urdu poets of the twentieth century, as cultural advisor to the Ministry of Culture and the Ministry of Education in 1972.

In 1978, after Bhutto is hanged under Zia's orders, Faiz leaves Pakistan. Zia establishes martial law and Islamic rule. Saris, considered Indian (un-Islamic), are banned by Zia's regime for public performances, talks, and other events. All protests are violently subdued. The people of Pakistan have no means to protest the imposition of a strict Islamic rule, which includes the banning of most poetry, music, and arts. True to his art, Faiz pens his famous protest poem, "Hum dekhenge" (We will see) in response to the military rule in his country.

In 1986, two years after Faiz's death that was unrelated to the protests, singer Iqbal Bano arrives in Lahore's Alhamra Arts Center, wearing a black sari. To celebrate Faiz's birthday, she sings his ghazals and nazms and reads his poetry. His poems, banned from being recited in public by Zia, held a mesmerizing power. There isn't a video recording of that night, but when Bano sings "Hum dekhenge," the entire auditorium erupts in cries of "In-quilab, Zindabad," which loosely translates as "may the revolution prosper." A technician at Alhamra makes an audio recording of that song, in which the audience's voices can be heard. According to Faiz's grandson, who attended that night, the loudest cheers are when she sings the following verse.[25]

Sab taj uchale jaayenge
sab takht giraaey jaayenge

All crowns will be flung
All seats [of power] will be brought down

That same night, many organizers' homes are raided by Zia's men, looking for any recordings of subversive music and poetry. Anticipating the crackdown, a copy is smuggled out to Dubai and distributed. Since then, "Hum dekhenge" is a battle cry in most student-led marches in South Asia.

What is the essence of this poem that continues to enthrall student revolutionaries? "Hum dekhenge" uses traditional Islamic imagery even though Faiz's religious ties were tenuous at best. But his poem obliquely attacks General Zia's dictatorship, calling for a revolution to establish democracy in Pakistan again.

Jab zulm-e-sitam ke koh-e-giraan,
rui ke tarah udh jaayenge
Hum mehkoomon ke paaon tale,
yeh dharti dhad dhadkegi

When the oppressor will push us down
Like cotton balls we will fly
Under this nation's people's feet
The earth will vibrate

The university protestors in India against CAA and NRC also sing this song. Online, there are many images of students sitting with their professors, singing the song with a passion only young idealists have. On December 17, 2019, students at the prestigious engineering school Indian Institute of Technology Kanpur in the state of Uttar Pradesh protest peacefully in solidarity with the Jamia students in New Delhi. As in many such protests since early December, the students sing Faiz's "Hum dekhenge." These are the words that ring throughout the campus:

Jab arz-e-khuda ke kaabe se
sab but uthwaaye jaayenge
Hum ahl-e-safa mardood-e-haram
masnad par baithaye jaayenge

When from Kaaba [the abode of God]
all idols will be removed
Then we the faithful, who were debarred
    from sacred places
Will be placed on the royal seat

The next day, faculty member Vashi Sharma officially lodges a complaint that the song provokes anti-Hindu sentiments. His reasoning is that a call for all idols to be removed makes this is an anti-idol poem and therefore anti-Hindu.[26] Such is the paranoia of nationalists, assuming the country is being taken over by Islamists. But Faiz's poem embraces the powerless; his point is not that images of the gods should be destroyed but that anyone in power who believes that he should be idolized like a god should be removed. Such is the paranoia of Hindu nationalists, assuming the country is being taken over by Islamists. That Faiz is an atheist, a communist, and most certainly a liberal secular poet is lost on those who look to find Islamic terrorism everywhere. If all you have is a hammer, everything looks like a nail.

IIT Kanpur's committee had retracted the investigation into Faiz's words in the poem by January 3, 2020. Instead, the leadership at the school now stated that they would examine the legitimacy of the protest itself, including inflammatory actions and posts.[27] While poetry fuels protests, institutions in India either are now afraid of the repercussions of not aligning with the nationalistic government (should they support the students) or are in fact aligned with the Hindutva regime. Although the schools may support the students, they are actively stepping back from taking a stance that could be construed by the government as anti-Hindu. Fleetingly, the power of poetry won that round, even as institutions are aligning with nationalism and the government.

· · · · · · · · · · · · · · ·

December 31, 2019, is a cold night in Delhi. The women of Shaheen Bagh sit in protest on the streets at the border of Noida and Delhi, cradling cups of hot tea and shivering under blankets.[28] Most of these women are uneducated homemakers—and poor. All are activists. And most of them are Muslim.

"I won't leave this country, and I don't want to die proving I am Indian," says ninety-year-old Asma Khatun.[29] She hasn't left the site in days.

While the CAA amendment targets Muslims, the protestors are homemakers, grandmothers, harried mothers of young children. Shaheen Bagh becomes a site of inclusivity and unity, beyond religion. The cause has converted the lower-middle-class and poor neighborhood into a beacon of idealistic protest. What started in Northeast India, then traveled to the capital city's universities, is now led by ordinary citizens. For more than three weeks, in the middle of a harsh Delhi winter, these homemakers and day laborers sit at this vigil in protest of the CAA amendment.

Shaheen Bagh may be the equivalent of a ghetto in the West, but now the ideologies of people at different economic levels slowly align. Students, activists, and concerned citizens from other neighborhoods filter into Shaheen Bagh to show their solidarity. This is how revolutions happen in a sit-in protest, a dharna, as it is called in Hindi.

The women sit on rugs and carpets on the road, blocking the six-lane highway to New Delhi. Children join their parents in this protest, elders lead. Religious divisions fade, everyone protests what is unfair at a human rights level.

. . . .

On the first Sunday of 2020, Jawaharlal University student union president Aishe Ghosh appears on camera, blood dripping down her face.[30] "I have been brutally attacked," she says, eyes blinking without her glasses, the blood from her head wound no doubt disorienting her. As she is being taken to the hospital, she tells the media how she was attacked and how no one came to help.

Social media reports accurately and inaccurately note how the thugs were able to enter the campus. Police teams were unable to enter the campus, however, prohibited by the college administration, which didn't want students to be policed. It is being broadcast that the left-leaning group that Ghosh belongs to and Akhil Bharatiya Vidyarthi Parishad, the nationalist Hindu student group on campus, were in conflict, leading to a two-hour riot-like atmosphere in New Delhi's premier educational institution. Then they say Ghosh injured herself to make it seem like an attack. In the world of WhatsApp and Twitter, a guess becomes conviction becomes truth and is magnified as such in seconds.

But in Shaheen Bagh, the protestors aren't the young idealists. Bilkis Bano, an eighty-something grandmother and part of the Shaheen Bagh Dadis, or Grandmothers of Shaheen Bagh, sits in protest, saying, "We are not scared, Allah is with us . . . we elected you, we will dethrone you."[31]

The "you" in this statement refers to Modi, the current prime minister of India. According to the progovernment propaganda machinery, Bilkis is a paid protestor anointed by the activists. She reacts in the way only grandmothers can—a YouTube video shows her saying "we will bring you down, we are not afraid of you. Allah is our protector."[32] She looks directly at the camera addressing the prime minister. After protesting the CAA for a hundred days, Bilkis is considered one of *Time* magazine's "100 Most Influential Persons of 2020."[33]

Close to the protest area, on the highway connecting New Delhi to the satellite town of Noida where the women sit for a third of a year, is a small café called Cafe Temptation. This coffee house has become the protest spot to be in during breaks in the cold Delhi winter. Run by Kavita, while her sister, Vandana, tends the coffee station. The café has seen many singers, activists, and well-known personalities come through its doors. The later you go, the larger the crowd.[34] As with everything else in Delhi neighborhoods, this small coffee house is as Westernized as it can be in an Indian lower-middle-class neighborhood. Instagram posts show the walls with quotations such as "The Best Time Is Coffee Time" and "The Day Should Start with Coffee and End with Ice-Cream."[35] Photos of actors of yesteryear such as Nafisa Ali, former ministers such as Salman Khurshid, and contemporary singers such as Saba Azad are all over the café's social media handle. Very rarely is there a photo of chai, even though that is what brings protestors and activists together.

In Shaheen Bagh, chaiwalas wander through Delhi's coldest winter in a century with hot tea in huge metal kettles and plastic cups to pour them into. Protests and poetry align with pekoe. The dharna lasts a hundred days. A hundred days later, the pandemic roars into the country. The government uses that as the reason to shut down all gatherings, including the Shaheen Bagh protest area. By the end of 2020, when the protestors are mostly absent, Cafe Temptation announces on social media that food will be available at 25 percent discount.

. . . .

Aishe is featured in the *New York Times* within days—the West likes a female activist who can speak English.[36] The West also loves Bilkis, a grandmother, illiterate and old as she may be, because her passionate activism transcends regions, generations, and language.

Even though the Shaheen Bagh area was cleared out in March 2020 and all gatherings banned, the protest by ordinary citizens was considered the first successful one in twenty-first-century India, primarily because the cause was greater than the housewives protesting. They raised their voices for the right to Indian citizenship on behalf of future generations, making this a uniquely altruistic fight for social justice.[37]

. . . .

These days I select coffee the way Baba used to select tea. I have gone to Guatemalan coffee farms and Ugandan coffee groves to smell the coffee roasting. I use my nose and my gut, much as Baba used to. We didn't have formal training in how to select what we liked, but food is a sensory love, in my opinion. You either know or you don't. Padma Lakshmi calls her sensitive palate that of a "super taster." She is aware of tastes and flavors that ordinary people may not be.[38] I don't think my method is that sensitive, but I'd like to think I have trained my palate. I can select the base and deep flavors in particular medium-roast coffees from Ugandan, Costa Rican, or Honduran farms, expertly use a French press for my morning cup, and select the right beans for my palate to be shipped to me from Leap Coffee, the local Carlsbad café that has now moved to Sabre Springs, another northeastern neighborhood in San Diego, during the pandemic. Leap's roaster selects the best African and Latin American coffee beans for me, sending me a note each time saying, we know you love this, and we agree with your choice.

Every month, as with the much-awaited Makaibari tins traveling from the mountains to the dry land in Delhi, I wait for my tiny shipment from the roasters to reach my house near the San Diego border with Mexico. I always finish the bag too soon and then anxiously wait a few days in between for the next shipment of small batch, vacuum-sealed bags. Those few days, I miserably scrape by with store-bought beans, cursing my greediness in the early part of the month, when I added an extra spoonful to the morning pot of coffee.

A dear friend, Halina, recently asked me whether I was doing with coffee what my father did with tea.

"What do you mean?" I ask.

"Isn't it interesting how you actively follow the coffee bean, select a particular blend, focus on the geography, looking for that subtle flavor. And you evangelize about that coffee from those particular roasters!"

I do prefer a Costa Rican single-origin coffee from the Palmichal mountain region. I also love Leap's method of roasting, which lends a light crispness to the sweetness of this coffee. With my permanence or semipermanence in a country that wakes up to coffee, I have adopted rituals that are American, perhaps global. But I also have inserted my Bengaliness into how I select it.

Perhaps this is another way I'm adopting and adapting while still holding onto the land I come from. Perhaps my passionate proclamations of Leap coffee's having the best medium-roast beans is a way of transforming myself into my Baba, when he proclaimed his love for Makaibari.

. . . .

A couple of years ago, when I visited India, I went on a road trip because I have never done one as an adult in the country that's mine.

I head to Jaipur and to a small railway town called Bandikui with a dear friend. We stop at a roadside dhaba, a diner. I try to recreate what I left, when I left India in 1993, hoping I'll get those years back.

"Rajan, chai, let's get kulhad chai," I nudge him, speaking Hindi to remind myself that I am still a Delhiite, even though home is a coastal town in America.

We ask for kadak chai, strong tea. The owner brings two small clay cups filled with milky gunpowder tea. It's buraada chai, used primarily as the transport medium for other spices, such as cardamom, ginger, and cloves. This is not the tea I grew up with. This certainly isn't Makaibari first flush.

The tea is deep brown, lightened with thick full-fat camel milk. It is what Baba told us never to drink. "That isn't tea. Tea is what comes from Darjeeling. Fresh, first flush."

When my friend says, "Achcha nahi laga," I protest, lying. "No, no, it's very good."

I sip the unfamiliar tea. I don't fit in here in many ways. Coffee is what I should be drinking, I think.

I sip it again. The smell of clay and the ginger boiled in the thick liquid reminds me of our train trips from New Delhi to Kolkata every summer on the Rajdhani Express. I may not fit in here in many ways, but look, here I do.

"Very good," I repeat, when I mean it.

CHAPTER 9

....

Memory and
What Makes a Family

After I move back to San Diego in 2014, the biggest challenge I have is my memory. I remember stories, episodes, and events from decades ago in clear detail. How people said what they did, what they were wearing, what I was doing, where we were. Didi's memory is even better than mine. It must be a Ghosh sisters thing, but yes, I have a memory that may keep me living through the past almost decade that I now acknowledge as trauma. It's what my memory holds onto from my dead marriage and its aftermath that I'm fearful of. But then, as Joan Didion said in *Blue Nights,* "Memory fades, memory adjusts, memory conforms to what we think we remember."

I have to be careful when I talk about my history and where I come from—what am I *choosing* to remember? This is tricky because the memory cells adhere to what they want to. It may be the truth in my mind, but mostly it's the truth in *my* heart. I will hold on to that.

....

When Baba died in 2004, the neighbors made sure to ask Ma what happened.

"How did he look that evening?"

"Was he happy and content?"

"Then what happened that night?"

When did Ma wake up to hear Baba struggling to breathe?

"And then what happened?"

When she screamed at him saying, "Shono, ki holo? Ki holo?" and Baba raised his hand signaling, wait, wait, give me a minute, and then he fell back on the bed, what did she do?

"Then what happened?"

"Then what happened?"

The neighbors asked over and over, "Mrs. Ghosh, Sila di, what did you do? Did you call for help? Did you call your doctor? What did you do?"

I remember them asking Ma and Ma responding. "'Yes,' he said. 'Wait,' he whispered, 'daaraao, daaraao,' and then his body hit the bed hard. He fell back on his pillow. I tried to call the next-door neighbors, but I forgot their number. I am a math teacher, numbers are what I do. That night I forgot the number. I don't know how long I looked through the notebook to find it. I tried to wake him up till the neighbors came with the doctor, but he didn't get up. He didn't get up."

I remember sitting at the dining table watching Ma in her chair repeating herself as if it were a chant that would soothe her shell-shocked mind. I remember feeling rage at the neighbors. How dare they make her go through this? Why do they ask the same questions? Why is Ma answering them?

Week after week, the neighbors came, asking the same questions. Ma had the same answers. Over and over. And then slowly, Ma had her routine.

Now when she woke up, the nurse that Didi and I employed to help her made her toast and tea. Then she walked up and down the hallway, lifting her arthritic feet one after another—her exercise to keep up her waning physical mobility. For her mental mobility, she showed the nurse what to cook, told the maid what to clean. She ate lunch, made calls to relatives, some friends, then napped in the afternoon, went for a walk in the park in the evening, and watched TV in the evening for as long as her tired eyes would let her. Then she ate her dinner, and the nurse helped with her medicines before tucking her in bed, pulling the heavy but warm and inviting lep over her bony torso. Ma's rituals after Baba left us became routine, a habit, as if she had lived like that for years. Soon she didn't talk about that night in October 2004, the last night of Durga Puja, when she lost her partner of nearly five decades. Instead, her conversations were about Baba doing something to irritate her or buying her the best handloom sari or a trip they took together. Her memories were happy ones.

I didn't—and neither did Didi—relive or talk about when we got the news. Nor did we talk with each other about what happened. Ma got over the trauma faster than we did. It's not that she wasn't sad. It's just that she used rituals and repetition to create a new normalcy in her life. It's been fifteen years for me. I am still trying to live without Baba. I'm still living in that Sunday afternoon when his neighbor called me in San Diego, saying, "Your father is dead."

It was late at night in India when the neighbor called me midafternoon in San Diego that October Sunday. I remember I was wearing a white T-shirt and this pair of jeans with a stripe running along the front. I remember I was to go for a job interview to the Bay Area the next day. I canceled the flight, leaving a shaky voice mail that I'd love to interview at a later date if I could get an opportunity again but that I had to go back because Baba was gone.

That's the problem when you're told you have a photographic memory—you revel in it as if it's an advantage. It's not. It means even when you want to forget, you cannot. Grief and the trauma of grief become part of that memory.

But I remember and I remember well, which also means that I need to create new memories, good ones, to imprint and take over the bad ones. It's a conscious effort for me. If the brain is a computer and the recesses of the brain a hard drive, I need to overwrite code to refresh it, imprint a newer code in a brain that remembers too much.

After staying in a rental cottage behind a rich couple's mansion for two years, I finally complete the divorce process. I move into my house near Old Town San Diego in 2016. It is the first space that is mine, truly mine—not

Ma's, Baba's, nor is it the Maryland house that was bought for my now ex and his family. I decide I have to create events, happiness, joys, rituals, and memories here. It is up to me.

. . . .

We Ghoshes aren't religious, though we love traditions such as Durga Puja, the festival celebrating the goddess Durga, avatar of Sati and Kali, coming home to earth from the Himalayas where she stays with Shiva, her husband. It's a Bengali festival, filled with seven days of food in multicolored cloth top pandals in neighborhood parks brightly lit with generator-assisted electric connections, music blaring from loudspeakers, aroti (felicitating the goddess with dhunuchi, coconut-camphor lit lamps, dancing to the dhaak drums), new clothes, plays, and all-night jaatraas (multiact plays). Durga Puja in C.R. Park and our childhood are what my memories are made of.

But in America, no one except for Bengalis know what it is. The puja in Delhi used to be very different from that in Kolkata. It may have now become commercialized with fancy singers showing up to sing a song or two, and the food stalls may be more North Indian than Bengali, but a Delhi puja isn't what it is in America either. I haven't gone to one in decades. Every year, however, Didi and her husband try to go to Durga Puja in the New England region. Organized by motley puja committees of Bengalis who had left India decades ago, each Bengali holds this celebration as a representation of what life used to be when they left home. Didi sends me photos of the two of them—he in a silk FabIndia kurta with jeans, she in a bright South Indian silk sari. They try to hold on to the rituals that were part of our lives in India when we were young. But we know it's not the same.

I consider celebrating Durga Puja—and can't think how I would celebrate it in my house. I don't know the prayer hymns, the songs, or how to pray. The Ghosh daughters haven't been taught that, nor do we want to be part of a ritual we don't believe in.

I settle on Diwali. The Festival of Lights. A Hindu festival, it celebrates the victory of good over evil—of Ram returning home to Ayodhya with his wife, Sita, and brother Lakshman after fourteen years of vanvaas, banishment to the forest by his father's third and beloved wife. While exiled, Sita is kidnapped by Raavan, the king of Lanka, and a fight over the girl ensues. Using the help of a super-monkey army led by Hanuman, Ram is victorious, killing Raavan, and his exile over, he returns home with his wife. Good wins over evil.

There are many problematic parts to this mythological story. That Sita needed rescuing. That Raavan, also known as an erudite man, needed to be killed.[1] That he kidnapped Sita, given that he did so because Ram and his brother had brutally chopped off Raavan's sister Shoorpanakha's ears and nose after she had lusted for Ram. A simple "No, I'm not interested, I'm married" might have sufficed. The violence against women in this Hindu epic isn't lost on me.

We never celebrated Diwali for what it represented to Hindus, because religion and blind faith weren't how we were brought up. It was always Ma asking us to question what we had been taught. But, but. Diwali, when the people of Ram's kingdom lit lamps to guide him back home and then set off fireworks to celebrate his victory alongside food—and lots of it—that I am good with.

In 2016, when I move into my home next to Old Town, I decide I will make my own Diwali. My own festival of lights.

. . . .

2019 November. Lucky from Carlsbad's Punjabi Tandoor shows up early with metal trays laden with food. While the Festival of Lights celebration is one where food is center stage in my house, it is the one time I don't cook. I order the best Punjabi food I can find in San Diego from the Sainis. Lucky's wife, Kamaljeet, and his sister, Satwinder, accompany him, giggling shyly when I offer them the naru I just made.

"Ji nahi," Satwinder makes a face, "I hate sweets."

"That's not an excuse," I scold her and pack some for the family. The girls take the box grudgingly but with a smile. This is after all, an Indian thing. When an elder thrusts food on you, you have to take it because you've been brought up with manners. I also realize I am their elder. In India, I'd proudly wear the honorific of an "aunty." A cool aunty, but aunty nonetheless.

Lucky sets up the burners and the food next to it. "The naan is hot, so you can leave it in the oven at 200. The rest of the food can be heated when the guests come. Enjoy—and happy Diwali!"

He leaves, his beard long, his turban thick, with the swagger of a young man. I have known that family for over seventeen years. I guess this too is how one creates family.

That evening I wear a sari—one of Ma's Benarasi silks. I feel close to her when I do. I can feel her in it. Every year, every Festival of Lights, I wear another sari of Ma's. I know she is enjoying this with me.

I invite everybody I know. This hasn't been done without thought. This is the first house that's mine. Mine. And the dog's. I want this celebration to be that of life itself. A new evening of welcoming and wishing each other well. My colleagues from pharmaceutical companies, biotech startups, my work team, department heads. Their spouses. Their children. The barista from the café where I spent every weekend when the divorce took all joy out of me, and he made me lattes with Ganesh designs to make me feel better. The barista's friend, the cotton candy girl with the pink hair, who made whiffs of fluffed sugar with organic food coloring and flavor and told me she didn't need payment so long as she could eat my food. The chef who made me egg sandwiches with extra avocado every weekend I spent in the café in Del Mar during the divorce. The hair stylist who held me quietly in her salon as I let myself break down with tears rolling down my face as I told her how I compiled a list of all the jewelry Ma and Baba gave me and sent it to my now ex so he could confirm I wasn't stealing from him.

The children mill around cotton candy girl, waiting for the endless supply of sugar and the subsequent high. My friends for decades, silent supporters of my life, my world. My neighbors. Their children. Friends of friends. Everyone I know. Everyone is invited—the house is full. Exactly how I want it to be.

The food is what it always is—chicken tikka masala, samosas, dal makhni, spinach paneer, cauliflower, raita. Standard buffet fare but made with love and extra special. Dessert is my naru, my nod to my family, and gulab jamun, large, syrupy-sweet, deep-fried paneer balls of goodness that only Punjabi Tandoor can bring me.

Then we have poetry. That isn't a Diwali norm, but in my house it is. Poetry from Tagore to Shakespeare to Warsan Shire. We all have to recite a poem, a joke, a song, something.

"Madhu, you really make us work for our food, don't you?" they grumble.

But everyone comes prepared with their contribution—it's become an annual event that we all look forward to. They leave with a small token: a box of chocolates, a snarky Post-it pack, a notebook. No one comes empty-handed, nor do they leave empty-handed.

Afterward, the core group of friends fold the chairs and then the tables. Clean off the crumbs and sauces, throw away the trash, then start the dishwasher. I don't have to do anything except pack leftovers that they can take home. Before they leave, they light a candle, wish each other well, a ritual we've created over the years. There is a calm routine to this—we all are there for each other, it is the Festival of Lights, and this is what friends do. Be there.

Every year during Diwali, I am reminded of how one can create one's family, when the family one was born into is gone. Society doesn't give enough credit to friendships that are sometimes closer than family, nor does it give friends the respect we give to spouses. Every Diwali is my unproblematic Thanksgiving.

The memories are happy because I choose them to be.

. . . .

By July 2020, I am sure the Festival of Lights will have to be on pause in the fall. But then, everything is on pause while we all try to survive. How to create new memories when time is at a standstill?

I spend 2020 at home, much like everyone else. After watching many alien invasion movies, it's ironic that the alien that finally does invade the world is not visible to the eye and yet can take over a human hosts in a matter of days, incapacitating and killing them by suffocation. Lungs of COVID-19 patients who died look ravaged, destroyed. It reminds us of the Great Influenza of 1918, an H1N1 strain thought to be from avian flu, which was very infectious from the start, but as it mutated into four strains, it became deadlier with each iteration.[2] More than 3 to 6 percent of the global population was decimated by the flu pandemic of 1918. It lasted two years. I know history and have also worked in infectious disease diagnostics. I stay home, and when I walk the dog, I mask up.

There is no Diwali to be celebrated in 2020. I wait. Perhaps what the Great Pause teaches me is the patience I never thought I needed to have. I wait.

. . . .

2019 Letter to My Now Ex That I Never Sent

Dear now ex,
    It's Diwali today
        the Festival of Lights to non-Indians
            We call it that when they ask us
Oh hey, what is this lovely festival with lights?
Is it the same one as the one with colors?
            and we say, no, it's not. That's Holi, a spring festival
this is Diwali, the festival when good vanquishes evil
    and we eat a lot
        We smile at each other, our own private joke

The first year when we celebrated
    the Santa Ana winds pushed the fires to our valley, so
close that I inhaled the smoke and inhaled the ash of dread
        It took me a decade to realize the man I married
didn't exist

I spent years to prove
        that he did
It took me even longer
           to leave

Sometimes I wake up and reach out across the bed
              because you and I never slept apart when we weren't fighting
I used to hold your thumb like a child when I would sleep
      you used to let me

That first year the fires came close
      to the street north of us
         and stopped
As if warning me that it could get worse

It did

Today is Diwali
         I am in a house far south of those apartments
      Cookie cutter
        you used to call them
      I am now close to the ocean and
           my house is on a hill
When I reach across the bed
        the Dalmatian groans out her protest
           Unlike you, she doesn't like
      being touched in her sleep

Today is Diwali
        All my friends will return
          I will feed them like it's a wedding
we will wish each other happy Diwali like
          we know what that means

I will wear a sari
        it's one of the few days I do anymore
Everyone will say, oh, how pretty
          Thank you, I'll reply

Once they help clean up some, I will say, leave, it's okay
They will
      After they leave, I will clean up the place
      Put away the candles
           turn off the string lights
                Tupperware the leftovers—
          freeze the dessert

I will clean my face
        and wear my old pajamas
           The same ones I bought after you left me
The ones that made me feel good
           when I hit "buy"
        on that website that charges too much for desi clothes
        I will wear those pajamas
            call the dog to bed
we will lie down
        and I will turn off the light

Dear now ex,
     I wish you a very happy Diwali

....

CHAPTER 10

The Rituals
of the Great Pause

According to the 2009 study published by the *European Journal of Social Psychology*, it takes eighteen to 254 days to form a habit. And it takes sixty-six days for a new habit to become automatic.[1] In 1960, Maxwell Maltz estimated that it takes a minimum of twenty-one days.[2] Since the book became a bestseller, ordinary people have assumed it takes about three weeks to form a new habit. In reality, it takes much longer and is much more personalized and variable. And while Maltz's theory has been debunked multiple times by various scientists, the attractiveness of a three-week habit-forming rule continues to stay strong.

When the first COVID-19 case is confirmed in the United States in January 2020, the patient had traveled to Wuhan, China, then back to Washington State, where he received care around January 15, 2020.[3] After that, in less than six weeks, the first nontravel related case was documented.[4] In twelve months, the death toll in America is 437,000, with more than twenty-six million positive cases. By March 19, 2020, the first statewide lockdown is established in California, where I live.[5]

By that date, I have already asked my team to stay home with their families. "Hunker down, family comes first," I say sagely, with more wisdom than I possess in March 2020. Having worked in respiratory viruses and knowing what a pandemic could look like, I reiterate, "It doesn't make sense to expose yourself or your family to this virus." We don't know how dangerous it could be or would be. It is a virus with a still unknown infection rate.

We are not asked to change our habits; rather, it is *demanded* of us—going out, meeting people, sending children to school, day care, grocery shopping, medical visits, engaging with strangers—everything is transformed in less than forty-eight hours. Habits formed over decades are abruptly put on hold. The difference between continuing and stopping is being infected with the virus and possibly dying. The entire world falls into the Great Pause, waiting for what we considered normal in January 2020 to return. As I write this, it has been forty-seven weeks since I have hugged a human.

What no one discusses but everyone complains about is that it takes America about forty-eight hours, not twenty-one days, to create a new habit. Because if we don't, the virus that came in as an unwanted guest will take over everything that we took for granted.

. . . .

The year before, I travel so much that my body and mind are exhausted to a point where I cannot recognize myself. All that travel is primarily for work—in 2019 I am working for the world's largest biotech company. It isn't just travel—it is a vicious flying-eighteen-hours-for-a-three-hour-meeting, then back home for half a day, and then off in the other direction for a five-hour meeting. Corporate travel is fun for those who are new to the job. For the rest of us, it is a relentless parade of waiting in lobbies, airport terminals, hotel rooms, haggling for seat upgrades, TSA PreCheck and Global Entry priority boarding notices, flight announcements, and delays, stamps on passports, customs, scrutiny, waiting at the luggage carousel if it's a longer trip, Lyft or Uber rides, and back to empty rooms in high-rise hotels.

The Great Pause is a welcome relief for me. It is certainly a joyous time for the dog because now she has me to herself, even if I am glued to a laptop screen for most of the day. At least I am home. The pandemic teaches us to look for joy when there is none, patience when it's fleeting and hard to come by, peace when surrounded by fear.

Food writer and photographer Nik Sharma says, "If your experiment works for the first time, then you're screwed."[6] As a former molecular biologist, he understands that what works in the lab can be translated into what happens in food. When I speak with him, almost nine months into the pandemic, he laughs. "Oh, I mess up every day! I feel one learns so much if you fail in your recipe-preps. That way, just like experiments, you can make it right and robust."

Like most Indian children, Nik loved Rooh Afza.[7] Created by Hakim Majeed in 1906 and based on Unani medicinal herbs and flavors, the dark pink, rose-flavored syrup was created to help cool and hydrate people in the hot Delhi summers.[8] A truly Indian Gatorade. In an effort to absorb the goodness of the rose flavor, Nik added the concentrated syrup to rice to make a sweet, gooey inedible goop.

"Ah, but I've made worse," he laughs on the phone when I ask him about his culinary failures. "I managed to burn tea!"

"What do you mean?"

"Oh, you know, same as the rooh afza situation. I thought if I boil the tea beyond what we do normally, it would concentrate the flavor. But over-boiling it meant that the leaves burnt in the saucepan."

The bottom line is food writers, chefs, and cooks aren't scared of rituals or new endeavors—the biggest ritual is creating actions that turn into habits even when one is afraid of failure.

• • • • • • • • • • • • • •

1977. In our I Block house, sholosho baaro, Baba started a vegetable garden. These days, I talk about that garden to anyone and everyone because what we grew those two years is what my childhood is made of: capsicum, eggplant, loofah, long beans, squash blossoms.

Baba used to say, "Bujhli to, in my desh, everything was bigger. Better." For him, desh remained what's now Bangladesh. Desh, for me, will always be India.

I realize I speak like Baba to anyone who will listen to me about my childhood. That garden in I Block, C. R. Park, had the best vegetables I've ever eaten. I dream about that garden almost daily. It has been four decades since we left that wraparound garden. And yet. And yet.

One almost always goes back to what's most comfortable. That garden is my place of peace.

．．．．．．．．．．．．．．．

March 2020. The world settles down to wait. For us, the world is the American one. We haven't learnt from the three months China was on lockdown. We made fun of Chinese families dancing in front of their televisions to music, saying, "That will never happen to us." We celebrated Italians singing opera from their balconies, creating music through their windows in multistory apartment buildings. We said, "Oh, look at them, they still show their culture and art in a pandemic. How artistic, how romantic!" Even in a pandemic, we judge and grade different countries in a manmade hierarchy of class and culture.

In America, do we learn from previous global experience? No. We create our own pandemic story. The world for us is a fight for toilet paper, for yeast, for the last egg on the shelf, the last Target, Trader Joes, Costco, and Walmart runs. Our fight is like post-Thanksgiving Black Friday sales mayhem. Why? Because this is a Western world, and when the capitalistic world is out of our control, we return to the rituals of fighting-in-a-land-of-paucity that created this country in the first place.

I joke with anyone who will listen, whoever is at the other end of the Zoom call: "I come from India. We managed for centuries without toilet paper. We have a process for butt cleaning, we will survive. Also, plant leaves work well!"

What I don't acknowledge is that I have lived in America longer than in my desh—this country is as mine as is the one I was born in. Toilet paper, much like eating with a fork and knife, is as much a part of me as it is for those who were born here. I too panic, even if more slowly than the rest, but panic I do. In April, a huge pallet of individually wrapped Georgia-Pacific rolls—a hundred of them—shows up on my front patio.

The masked Amazon deliveryman takes a picture of the huge cardboard box as proof and gives me an "Okay, so *you're* one of them" look.

It is week forty-seven as I write this. I am still using that toilet paper stash—which as Georgia-Pacific says, is perfect for camping, road trips, trailers, and for use when nothing else is available. I have become the type of American I used to roll my eyes at.

This is what I told Baba about Americans when I called him as a graduate student: "Baba, na, they focus only on the immediate. Their family. Their values. Their country. Their superiority. Their joy. Only that which is theirs is important." Of course, at that time I didn't know what I know now—I am referring to the wealthier Americans who mostly happen to be white and privileged.

I have become one of them.

. . . .

Most social media posts, besides panicking about the daily rise in the number of COVID-19–related deaths, infections, N95 masks, and COVID-19 variants, are focused on food. Bread in particular.[9] Not just any bread, but sourdough. It's also a consequence of scarcity. Everyone, meaning *everyone*, is baking bread because it needs time, which we didn't have previously, and now that's all we have. It takes flour, butter, oil, sugar, salt, yeast, and sometimes eggs—simple ingredients for a novice baker. Soon, as is expected, and in a time of intense social media as the sole interactive tool for most, one finds out that not only flour but eggs too are scarce. The world isn't ready for so many bakers baking all at once.[10]

Bakers bake sourdough during the pandemic because of a yeast shortage in the supermarkets. If yeast isn't available, then one can grow the bugs that exist in the air to help the bread rise. Sourdough is a home-science experiment that's also creative. It's something to look forward to. Something to feed the family. It's something to do.

The younger generations get almost all of their information online. The isolation experiment has now reached a grand scale. Even if we are physically alone, we are genuinely connected to a virtual online community through a screen and the touch of a few keys. The Gen Z, millennials, and even the younger Gen X (the group I belong to) have adapted to the virtual community easily because that may have been the only one we had. When we connect on social media, most connecting apps have now been identified as not really contributing to the "greater good" or to "social connections" as effectively as they had been purported to be. How they control our data—and, in effect, us—has been out in the open, and yet day after day we still log on. This is because when physical—and what we had considered normal—connection was so rudely eliminated by fear, social media finally became what it claimed it was there for: to connect us to what used to be. And what used to be normal and is now the best substitute for touch is social media and food. As for me, I devolve into snark.

I joke, "Good thing I don't have family. Good thing the parents are long gone."

Macabre humor keeps me sane. But I'm glad I don't have to worry about my parents' health thousands of miles away at this time. The dog keeps me sane. Didi is married to my friend and that they take care of each other—even though they are on the other side of America—keeps me sane. Simple texts from my neighbors and friends I've known for decades, just a simple "hi," keep me sane. Friday Zoom dinners with my friends, even when we repeat our stories, keep me sane.

I am—and have been—alone since 2012. This isn't new. I am also an introvert who can masquerade well as an extrovert. Staying alone with my thoughts is something I look forward to. My frenetic 2019 traveling now tells me the universe has asked me to stay home. And I do what I always do, I cook.

. . . .

Started during the George Washington—era as the first New England food company in America, King Arthur is one of the oldest flour companies in

North America.[11] It dramatically increases its production and packaging capabilities in March 2020. Flour is available because companies like this Vermont-based company have engaged with the community as a B Corp, with a twenty-four-hour baking hotline for novice bakers. Certified B corporations are organizations that work to reduce inequality, improve worker conditions, reduce poverty, and actively aim to produce a healthier environment and, in turn, a stronger community. These B Corps use profits and growth to ensure a better future for their employees and the community at large. King Arthur is one of them. The employee-owned company and its flour products become a lifeline during the Great Pause for millions of Americans, working toward a greater good that nobody anticipated would be needed in 2020.

I am not a flour person. I have gravitated to gluten-free for many reasons, mostly health-related. I focus on locally sourced vegetables and meat. Wheat flour isn't a necessary ingredient for me anymore. If anything, I can do the same with almond or mixed tapioca and cassava flour. I make mininaans with gluten-free flour from King Arthur, using with black onion seeds as garnish. I am sure others do too. My life becomes a daily exercise in what food will be easy to make but a joy to taste and to see and share, even if online.

The point isn't that extroverts or introverts don't know what to do—the point is, what do we have in our control when nothing is in our control? I realize the term "control" is also an interesting one. After all, there is nothing we can actually call control in our lives. We just like to believe we have some ability and choice in how we make our decisions.

· · · · · · · · · · · · · · ·

Unlike most of us, chef Maneet Chauhan thinks the pandemic has been good in that she's kept busy. Maneet and her husband, Vivek Deora, own the Chauhan Ale & Masala House and the Morph Hospitality Group in Tennessee.[12] She is dropping her child off to class when I speak with her.

"Arrey," she says, sprinkling Hindi words much as I would if I were speaking with a desi. "It's all good. We're busy with takeouts and socially

Gluten-free mininaan with onion seeds

distanced table dining. And my role as a mom never ends, so I haven't had time to think about what ifs."

Chef Chauhan has a large Punjabi personality, a laugh that captures hearts, and the can-do attitude of an intelligent, hardworking desi. About six years younger than me, she's still part of a generation of immigrants that's grateful and in awe of how far we've come and how good the experience has been.

I ask her the obvious question, "Why Tennessee?"

She laughs. "Southern folks are so keen to learn from us. And when we thought to take a chance—given that there were so many asking us to partner with them in the restaurant business—we told ourselves that we'll go back and forth to New York and manage to keep both lives going. I was pregnant with my son and my daughter was a baby. Everything was going according to plan."

"And then something changed that, didn't it?"

"Of course it did. My son!" she says, and I can almost see her eyes roll, a happy eye roll. "My son decided that the day of the restaurant opening would be the day he'd arrive early. And surprise, surprise, neither Vivek nor I could make it to our own restaurant's opening! But that made us realize that Nashville was asking us to be here, make this home. And we have."

The South has been good to Chef Chauhan—being a celebrity chef, a TV personality, and judge on *Chopped* has helped her business. Chef Chauhan, with her irrepressible enthusiasm about teaching her adopted townspeople easy lessons on Punjabi food and how to pair it with wines and beers they're used to. Her celebrity brings tourists from other Southern states to her restaurants and bars in the Nashville region. That she doesn't compromise on her in-your-face Punjabi cuisine, that she celebrates street foods such as chaat and highlights them on her menu tells us how far Indian food has reached within America, from a time when "curry" was a dirty insult, a common one thrown at children of desi immigrants in the '60s and '70s to the present, when it is celebrated as a cuisine packed with superfoods such as turmeric, ginger, cloves, and mango.

Chef Chauhan's steadfast focus on teaching the untaught about Indian food, which is a vast group of foods with distinct regional differences, brings hope that a good immigrant can be loud and brash and happy and *still* be celebrated in the food world. It's her brand of what a successful immigrant chef looks like, a Punjabi chef and a confident woman.

. . . .

An effect of cooking full-time at home is that we generate waste that truly isn't that. Social media posts crop up with garlic scapes, green onions, parsley, potatoes, squashes—seeds or roots or eyes of scraps of vegetables that were thrown into the soil and then grew into plants. If it's not sourdough, it's growing vegetables from scraps. I participate in that with an enthusiasm I didn't know I had in years.

Potato plants grow with a vengeance. Gardeners tell me that I cannot harvest them until the leaves die—the plants stay verdant for months. Green onions grow easily, and I harvest the stalks whenever I need a chive substitute. I have thrown leek bulbs in a soft felt planter that grow robustly without much tending.

I head to the Indian grocery store for a semiannual Indian spice and vegetable run. People aren't masked up there, there is no social distancing—it feels like returning to an India that I left in 1993, where rules are meant to be guidance and certainly never enforced. By mid-2020, I have reached a place of fear of an unknown virus and a place of outrage at people who don't listen to science, but I don't engage, nor do I ask anyone to mask up. Some wars aren't meant to be fought. At the store, I pick up a few taro roots, some tindora (ivy gourd) greens, a pound of one of my favorite vegetables, okra, and dash back out, my face masked, my hands gloved.

Once I return, I wash everything thoroughly, throw out the plastic wrap, vigorously scrub my hands and face before I chop most of the vegetables to cook later that day. I save the taro for another time. I spend an hour taking a hot shower, hoping I didn't bring the virus home.

. . . .

In his new house, Nik has a haphazard garden. It's not the manicured place that people think most food writers or personalities pose in, and he doesn't have the immaculate kitchen that we expect food writers, chefs, and photographers to have. Nik says the garden decided to grow that way, and he hasn't tried to change its organic fluidity. He brought vatana, or white dried peas, from the Indian grocery store, used his molecular and plant biology experience to germinate them, and now has a pea garden, mixed in with pollinating plants, including a Mexican marigold, long beans, and fruit trees. He did this in his earlier house, and he's done it again.

"I usually use what I grow," Nik says with pride.

Taro leaf

The pandemic means many of us are spending more time in the garden. On social media, I drolly call myself the Desi Pioneer Woman when I post an image of my paltry parsley, chives, leeks, mustard greens, and passion fruit.

. . . .

While I cook most of the vegetables from the Indian store, I don't remember the taro roots until a week goes by. By the time I see them in a bowl by the onions, green shoots are peeking through the hairy brown fibers coating the root.

That summer, I plant the accidentally sprouting taro roots between the tomatoes and the parsley. Within two weeks, the leaves pop out, unfurling like Japanese parasols. When I WhatsApp Didibhai a picture, her maid takes a look at the leaves and says, "Oh, choto kochu!" Apparently kochu can be two types—choto, the small hairy version of taro, and boro, large, the colocasia yam version. I had obviously forgotten the varieties.

"Be careful, the leaves can cause your throat to itch. Before you cook it, soak it in salt water."

Taro leaves, especially young ones, contain high concentrations of calcium oxalate.[13] The particulate matter leads to rashes and itching, usually when the leaves are eaten without treating them, sometimes even from just handling them. Boiling taro leaves in salt water or cooking them thoroughly is sufficient to reduce the effect of insoluble calcium oxalate. Besides the oxalate, the taro leaves contain polyphenols, which are known for their antioxidant properties.

In Hindi, this root is called arbi. I grew up calling it "colocasia" in English; taro is what people call it in America. There are a few different types of this root. The one I am growing now is ugly, small, knobby, and covered with brown fibrous hair. It is the king of vegetables—and a go-to easy-to-make dish in many Indian households. Taro root contains vitamin E and magnesium, along with being a good source of vitamin C and minerals such as Ca, Cu, Fe, K, Mg, Se, and Zn, along with beta carotene. The root is extremely fibrous and filling, enabling digestion with a low glycemic index.

My own desi philosophy is that when we grow roots and let the roots spread, and if the soil is life giving, we can live well. Be they taro or be they us. Roots, if strong, survive many a pause.

. . . .

If I want to make the curry a Bengali one, I can add mustard oil to boiled taro root, salt, and green chilies, for a simple boiled mash to eat with rice. Ma used to make a simple curry, but she's not here to tell me the recipe.

The internet, however, is my trusty friend. I decide to make a North Indian taro curry with the roots I grew in my yard.

. . . .

Nik's cauliflower-parmesan-sriracha pakoras are the exact opposite of trying to recreate memories of people long gone. While very American, these fritters are quintessentially desi, but with a dash of sriracha hot sauce and parmesan, which enables flavors never before experienced in Indian cuisine. Nik's confident perspective on what food means and a gay immigrant's statement on cooking is doing to Indian food what Chef Chauhan is continuing with her Punjabi fare and flair. What fascinates me about Nik's food and photography is the insertion of his brown hands in them—reminding all of us of the people behind the food, who are mostly nonwhite and who bring hints of their homeland with them.

DESI TARO ROOT CURRY (SERVES 2)

. . . .

6–8 medium size taro root bulbs
2 teaspoon turmeric powder
1 teaspoon cumin powder
1 teaspoon cumin seeds
½ cup shallots (or onions)
1 teaspoon chili powder
1 teaspoon grated ginger
2 teaspoons carom seeds

1 cup chopped tomatoes
1 teaspoon mango powder
1 teaspoon asafetida
Salt to taste
1 teaspoon lemon juice (optional)
Coriander leaves (chopped), as garnish

Boil the taro root bulbs (skin on) in a pressure cooker with salt, turmeric, and cumin seeds. Peel the skin and roughly chop up the white meaty flesh. In a separate pan, sauté turmeric, ground cumin, chili powder, and ginger along with ajwain, or carom seeds. Add chopped tomatoes with chopped shallots. Sauté for 4–5 minutes before adding in the chopped taro. Add more carom seeds and

*Me holding a bunch of parsley, rosemary, and
mustard greens during The Great Pause, 2021*

turmeric as needed. Season with amchur or mango powder and asafetida. Add salt to taste. Sprinkle water and lower flame. Cover the curry to cook another 4–5 minutes.

Before serving, add lemon juice (optional) and garnish with a few coriander leaves. Serve with rotis.[14]

....

I have grown mustard greens during this Great Pause and am waiting for more taro root, avocados, leeks, and tomatoes from my garden. I may not be Baba, and this isn't Baba's bountiful garden, but touching the leaves makes me feel as if I am back in sholosho baaro, C. R. Park.

The Bengali word for "again" is abaar. And the word for food is khabaar.

....

No wonder "again" remains part of "food" in Bengali, because khabaar means we bring it to our people abaar, again. And again. And again. Life has an interesting way of making us return back to shore, back to home. It is February 2021. Vaccines have rolled out. Some of us have received the first dose. Some of us wait. The restaurants open. Then close. Then open. Governments fall. Presidents change. We wait. And while we do, we create new habits.

These days I wake up and head to the yard to touch my plants to say, "Kaymon achcho?"

Baba said talking to plants gives them joy. There is as yet no conclusive scientific basis for that, but it can't hurt, can it?

These days, life is slower. And work is still frenetic. Then again, I watch the sun set from my window, the dog tells me she needs to sleep and I need to shut off work, and I do.

Sometimes, this is what we have. Sometimes, this will have to do. I will wait for the next Festival of Lights—it will be a celebration of good over evil. It will be joy, food, and love. But till then, I wait.

ACKNOWLEDGMENTS

Khabaar has been a team effort, decades in the making. Gratitude doesn't even begin to explain how I feel about the mentors, authors, and writing communities that helped it along.

Khabaar happened because of a secret online group of women and gender non-conforming writers. Special thanks to the forums on which *Khabaar* was conceptualized and where the book sold. I haven't met most of them, and yet they know me better than most—thank you! Thank you to my amazing FoodStory series editor, Nina Mukerjee Furstenau, for her quiet guidance; the University of Iowa Press, especially Susan Hill Newton, managing editor, for her behind-the-scenes leadership and advice; copyeditor Carolyn Brown for her amazing attention to detail and exceptionally great sense of humor; Allison T. Means, marketing director, for all her help, as well as the tremendously supportive press team, who have been only grace, patience, and joy. A special thank you to its director, James McCoy, for shaping *Khabaar* into what it is today. Dana Newman's quiet energy has kept me on track; thank you for being the agent I needed.

Over the years, editors shaped my work more than I ever imagined. Sari Botton, Melissa Chadburn, Christine Lee, Dinty Moore, Marisa Siegel, Snigdha Sur, Donna Talarico-Beerman, and Monet Thomas, salaam and shukriya for showing me how it's done. If any writer is reading this, please know that editors are lifesavers.

Early drafts of *Khabaar* were exhaustively read, reread, and constructively critiqued by amazing writers and dear friends, Halina Duraj and April Wilder. To the creatives who actively supported and championed my

Ma and Baba, ca. 1966

work, dhanyavaad. Thank you, Christina Adams, Kavita Das, Sayantani Dasgupta, Anjali Enjeti, Sonia Faleiro, Lisa Fugard, Ishay Govender, Julie Himes, Mira Jacob, Lacy M. Johnson, Jenny Lumet, Megha Majumdar, Huda Al-Marashi, Rahul Mehta, Nayomi Munaweera, Bedo Pain, Deesha Philyaw, Namrata Poddar, Sejal Shah, and so many more. The now defunct Book Works in Del Mar started my writing life in San Diego; thank you and we miss you, Milane Christiansen.

I relearned how to write in America—a very different proposition than what I was used to in India—from writing workshops and teachers who understood that South Asians are born storytellers, and we show *and* we tell. Romba nandri to the Sirenland family and Squaw, Tin House, and to Aspen Words friends for residencies, scholarships, classes, guidance, and the many different ways you all have shaped my writing life.

Dhanyavadalu to Adrienne Brodeur, Alexander Chee, Catherine Ryan Hyde, Michael Maren, Richard Russo, Dani Shapiro, the Shepards (Jim and Karen), Hannah Tinti, and Luis Alberto Urrea. Without you, this would be dust.

My extended #girlgab group has been a substitute for the family that's now gone, especially in this pandemic—you know who you are and twaada bahutaan dhanyavaad. My cheerleaders, advisors and family, Heather Dane, Marcie Frank, the spectacular Chiwoniso Kaitano, Caren Mair, Robert Saiz, Stacey Seeloff, Sarah Thyre, and Mia Vaughnes, tumhare hardam abhaari hain hum. Lookie what we did, Nancy Frank!

Shukran to the activist women in science, especially those of color who continue to work tirelessly for the next generation, and to the immigrants who bring their world to their adopted country—and how! Onek shubechcha and bhalobasha to Chittaranjan Park, my neighborhood in New Delhi, that has my heart as does America's Finest City, San Diego.

The family I was born into made *Khabaar*. For that I will be forever kritaartho to my parents, Hashi and Sila Ghosh, to my sister and brother-in-law, and to my cousin, Chhandasree Ghosh, keepers of stories. Finally, shokreeya to The Dalmatian, aka The Dog Who Adopted Me, who showed me what happiness should look like.

NOTES

·················

Author's Note

1. Joan Didion, *Blue Nights* (New York: Knopf, 2011).
2. Jumoke Verissimo, "On the Politics of Italics," *LitHub*, August 28, 2019, https://lithub.com/on-the-politics-of-italics/.
3. Khairani Barokka, "The Case Against Italicizing 'Foreign' Words," *Catapult*, February 11, 2020, https://catapult.co/stories/column-the-case-against-italicizing-foreign-words-khairani-barokka.
4. See Margot Harris, Palmer Haasch, and Rachel E. Greenspan, "A New Podcast Is Exploring the Reckoning That Happened at Bon Appétit. Here's How the Publication Ended Up in Hot Water," *Insider*, February 9, 2021, https://www.insider.com/bon-apptit-timeline-allegations-drama-culture-race-andy-alex-sohla-2020-6. See also Hannah Giorgis, "The Table Stays White," *Atlantic*, June 16, 2020, https://www.theatlantic.com/culture/archive/2020/06/bon-appetit-and-why-table-stays-white/613093/.
5. Sharanya Deepak, "There Is No Dalit Cuisine," *Popula*, November 20, 2018, https://popula.com/2018/11/20/there-is-no-dalit-cuisine/.

Chapter 1: Peyaara se Pyaar or the Love for Guava

1. Lorraine Boissoneault, "Literacy Tests and Asian Exclusion Were the Hallmarks of the 1917 Immigration Act," *Smithsonian Magazine*, February 6, 2017, https://www.smithsonianmag.com/history/how-america-grappled-immigration-100-years-ago-180962058/.
2. Richard A. Posner, "The Race against Race," *New Republic*, January 28, 2010, https://newrepublic.com/article/72808/the-race-against-race.
3. Karen Leonard, *Making Ethnic Choices: California's Punjabi Mexican Americans* (Philadelphia: Temple University Press, 1994), 23, 115.

4. S. K. Mitra, M. R. Gurung, and P. K. Pathak, "Guava Production and Improvement in India: An Overview," *Acta Horticulturae* 787, no. 4 (2008): 59–66, https://doi.org/10.17660/ActaHortic.2008.787.4.

Chapter 2: Maachher Bazaar, Fish for Life

1. Snehal Tripathi, "CR Park Throbs with Bengali Way of Life," *Hindustan Times*, August 11, 2016, https://www.hindustantimes.com/delhi/cr-park-throbs-with-bengali-way-of-life/story-v22yEjxyN8qEXU9RclvVqO.html.
2. Samin Nosrat, *Salt, Acid, Fat, Heat: Mastering the Elements of Good Cooking* (New York: Simon & Schuster, 4th ed., 2017).
3. Samin Nosrat, "ArtPower Presents Samin Nosrat," a conversation with Evan Kleiman, October 11, 2019, Balboa Theater, San Diego.
4. Samin Nosrat, "Mast-o Khiar (Persian Cucumber and Herb Yogurt) Recipe," *New York Times*, May 14, 2019.
5. Samin Nosrat, "Samin Nosrat's 10 Essential Persian Recipes," *New York Times*, May 14, 2019, https://www.nytimes.com/2019/05/14/dining/persian-food-recipes-samin-nosrat.html.
6. Y. A. El-Samragy, E. O. Fayed, A. A. Aly, A. E. A. Hagrass, "Properties of Labneh-Like Product Manufactured Using Enterococcus Starter Cultures as Novel Dairy Fermentation Bacteria," *Journal of Food Protection* 51, no. 5 (May 1988): 386–90, https://pubmed.ncbi.nlm.nih.gov/30978896/.

Chapter 3: Feeding the Future Ex-in-Laws . . .

1. Instagram hashtag, https://www.instagram.com/explore/locations/257448400/mr-and-mrs-mohgan-super-crispy-roti-prata/.
2. Koh Yuen Lin, "Taste Test: Mr Mohgan's Super Crispy Roti Prata vs His Ex-Assistant Cook's" *8 Days* (Singapore), December 2018, https://www.8days.sg/eatanddrink/restaurantreviews/taste-test-mr-mohgan-s-super-crispy-roti-prata-vs-his-ex-10983730.
3. US Citizenship and Immigration Services Guidelines, Optional Practical Training (OPT) for F-1 students, https://www.uscis.gov/working-in-the-united-states/students-and-exchange-visitors/optional-practical-training-opt-for-f-1-students.
4. Balaram Pradhan and Seema Godse Derle, "Comparison of the Effect of Gayatri Mantra and Poem Chanting on Digit Letter Substitution Task," *Ancient Science of Life* 32, no. 2 (October–December 2012): 89–92, https://www.ncbi.nlm.nih.gov/pmc/articles/PMC3807963/.

5. Instagram hashtag #mrandmrsmohgansupercrispyrotiprata, https://www
.instagram.com/explore/locations/257448400/mr-and-mrs-mohgan-super
-crispy-roti-prata/.

Chapter 4: In Search of Goat Curry

1. Ishay Govender-Ypma, "South African Bunny Chow: A Portable, Spicy Curry,
All Snug in Bread," *Food52* (blog), January 12, 2018, https://food52.com/blog
/21290-how-to-make-south-african-bunny-chow.

2. Alan Greenblatt, "Bunny Chow: South Africa's Sweet Sounding Dish Has a
Not-So-Sweet Past," *The Salt*, NPR, February 1, 2017, https://www.npr.org
/sections/thesalt/2017/02/01/511834972/bunny-chow-south-africas-sweet
-sounding-dish-has-a-not-so-sweet-past.

3. Sarah Khan, "In Durban, South Africa, 13 Curry Stops in 5 Days," *New York
Times*, October 23, 2015, https://www.nytimes.com/2015/10/25/travel/durban
-south-africa-restaurants.html.

4. Ishay Govender-Ypma, "The Brutal History of South Africa's Most Famous
Curry," *Munchies: Food by Vice*, November 11, 2017, https://www.vice.com/en
/article/qv3njv/the-brutal-history-of-south-africas-most-famous-curry.

5. "Yeh dosti hum nahi todenge," music director, R. D. Burman; singers, Kishore
Kumar and Manna Dey; lyricist, Anand Bakshi; from *Sholay* (Hindi), directed
by Ramesh Sippy, 1975, http://www.lyricsoff.com/songs/ye-dosti-hum-nahin
-todenge.html.

6. Lyrics in "Rote hue, aate hain sab," music director, Kalyanji Anandki, singer,
Kishore Kumar; lyricist, Anand; from *Muqaddar ka Sikandar* (Hindi), directed
by Prakash Mera, 1978, http://www.lyricsoff.com/songs/rote-hue-aate-hain
-sab.html.

7. "The Spice King," *Forbes*, July 26, 1998, https://www.forbes.com/forbes/1998
/0727/6202052a.html?sh=2b722ce032ae. See also Spice Emporium website,
https://www.spiceemporium.co.za/about-us/.

Chapter 5: When Indira Died

1. Prabhas K. Dutta, "The Last Day of Indira Gandhi," *India Today*, October 31,
2018, https://www.indiatoday.in/india/story/the-last-day-of-indira-gandhi
-1379440-2018-10-31.

2. William E. Smith, *Time Magazine*, November 12, 1984, "Indira Gandhi: Death
in the Garden," http://content.time.com/time/subscriber/article/0,33009
,926929-2,00.html.

3. Human Rights Watch, "India: Prosecute Those Responsible for 1984 Massacre of Sikhs," news column, New York, November 2009, https://www.hrw.org/news/2009/11/02/india-prosecute-those-responsible-1984-massacre-sikhs.

4. Patricia Gossman, *Punjab in Crisis: Human Rights in India*, Asia Watch Report (New York: Human Rights Watch, 1991), https://www.hrw.org/sites/default/files/reports/INDIA918.PDF.

5. Mohit Saggu, "7 Things You Need to Know about Operation Bluestar," *DNA*, June 6, 2014, https://www.dnaindia.com/india/report-7-things-you-need-to-know-about-operation-blue-star-1993952.

6. Prashant Bharadwaj, Asim Ijaz Khwaja, and Atif Mian, "The Big March: Migratory Flows after the Partition of India," Harvard Kennedy School Faculty Research Working Paper Series, June 2008, https://research.hks.harvard.edu/publications/getFile.aspx?Id=308.

7. "Who Are the Guilty? Causes and Impact of the Delhi Riots," *Economic and Political Weekly* 19, no. 47 (1984): 1979–85, http://www.jstor.org/stable/4373787.

8. Rahul Bedi, "Indira Gandhi's Death Remembered," London, BBC UK, November 2009, http://news.bbc.co.uk/2/hi/south_asia/8306420.stm.

Chapter 6: Dessert in Kolkata Summers

1. US Food and Drug Administration, "Overview of IVD Regulation," September 16, 2019, https://www.fda.gov/medical-devices/ivd-regulatory-assistance/overview-ivd-regulation.

2. US Food and Drug Administration, "Pre-Market Notification, 510k Submission Overview," March 13, 2020, https://www.fda.gov/medical-devices/premarket-submissions/premarket-notification-510k.

3. National Coalition Against Domestic Violence (NCADV), "National Statistics," Statistics, https://ncadv.org/statistics.

Chapter 7: Orange, Green, and White

1. Mayukh Sen, "Who Gets an Obituary?," *Eater*, May 1, 2020, https://www.eater.com/2020/5/1/21243344/garima-kothari-murder-press-coverage-bias-pandemic.

2. Stacey Feintuch, "Nukkad Brings Home-Style Indian Cuisine to Jersey City," Bestofnj.com, February 17, 2020, https://bestofnj.com/features/food/nukkad-brings-home-style-indian-cuisine-to-jersey-city/.

3. Garima Kothari, "These Apple Dumplings Completely Changed My View on Food," *Salon*, December 7, 2019, https://www.salon.com/2019/12/07/these-apple-dumplings-completely-changed-my-view-on-food_partner/.

4. Yelp review, Nukkad, Jersey City, New Jersey, 2020, https://www.yelp.com/biz
/nukkad-jersey-city-2. The restaurant has since been permanently closed.

5. Le Cordon Bleu, "Garima Kothari—Pastry Diploma 2013," interview with
Garima Kothari, https://www.cordonbleu.edu/paris/gareuma-kothary-pastry
-diploma/en.

6. Mark Lamport-Stokes, "Recovering Federer Upbeat for Indian Wells," *Reuters
Sports*, March 14, 2008, https://www.reuters.com/article/us-tennis-men-pacific
-federer-idUSSP7603720080315.

7. Ela Dutt, "Restaurant Owners Found Dead in Jersey City," *New India Times*,
April 26, 2020, https://www.newsindiatimes.com/restaurant-owners-found
-dead-in-jersey-city/. See also Kothari's breakingbread.co Instagram post from
New York City, with Madhur Jaffrey, June 2017, https://www.instagram.com
/p/BVo9HzrjWRz/.

8. Garima Kothari's breakingbread.co Instagram post from Cusco, Peru, June
2019, https://www.instagram.com/p/ByQgCqahqfs/.

9. National Coalition Against Domestic Violence, Domestic Violence in New
Jersey, fact sheet, 2020, https://assets.speakcdn.com/assets/2497/ncadv_new
_jersey_fact_sheet_2020.pdf.

10. Marilyn Baer, "Facts Revealed in Suspected Murder-Suicide," May 2, 2020,
https://hudsonreporter.com/2020/05/02/facts-revealed-in-suspected-murder
-suicide/.

11. Makaibari, http://www.makaibari.com/en/sustainable-tourism/homestay
-makaibari.aspx.

12. Narcissistic Personality Disorder, Symptoms and Causes, Mayo Clinic, https://
www.mayoclinic.org/diseases-conditions/narcissistic-personality-disorder
/symptoms-causes/syc-20366662.

13. "De Blasio Calls Stimulus Deal's Treatment of N.Y.C. 'Immoral,'" *New York
Times*, March 25, 2020, https://www.nytimes.com/2020/03/25/nyregion
/coronavirus-new-york-update.html.

14. Liz Robbins, "Rejuvenated Federer Returns to U.S. Open Final," *New York
Times*, September 6, 2008, https://www.nytimes.com/2008/09/07/sports
/tennis/07men.html.

15. Mayukh Sen, "Who Gets an Obituary?"

16. Mayukh Sen, "Restaurants Will Close—and What's Left Will Be Vanilla," in
"The Legacy of the Pandemic: 11 Ways It Will Change the Way We Live" series, *Vox*, April 22, 2020, https://www.vox.com/the-highlight/2020/4/16/212635
/coronavirus-covid--pandemic-legacy-quarantine-state-of-mind-frugality.

17. Sen, "Who Gets an Obituary?"

18. Ibid.

19. Shannon Thomas, *Healing from Hidden Abuse: A Journey through the Stages of Recovery from Psychological Abuse* (Tempe, Arizona: Mast, 2006), https://healingfrom hiddenabuse.com/.

20. "Chocolate Olive Oil Cake," https://www.nigella.com/recipes/chocolate-olive -oil-cake.

Chapter 8: Of Papers, Pekoe, Poetry, and Protests in 2019 India

1. Makaibari, http://www.makaibari.com/en/buy-tea/black.aspx?type3=3.

2. "What Is CAA?," *Times of India*, January 8, 2020, https://timesofindia.indiatimes .com/india/what-is-caa/articleshow/73153785.cms.

3. "Census of India, Literacy Rate, 2021," https://censusofindia2021.com/literacy -rate-of-india-2021/#Literacy_rate_of_India_2021.

4. Dexter Filkins, "Blood and Soil in Narendra Modi's India," *New Yorker*, December 2, 2019, https://www.newyorker.com/magazine/2019/12/09/blood-and-soil -in-narendra-modis-india.

5. UK Tea & Infusions Association, "Commercial Powerhouse, https://www.tea .co.uk/east-india-company.

6. Encyclopaedia Britannica, s.v. "Boston Tea Party," https://www.britannica.com /event/Boston-Tea-Party.

7. Arup K. Chatterjee, "How Chai Arrived in India 170 Years Ago," *Hindu*, August 18, 2018, https://www.thehindu.com/society/how-chai-arrived-in-india -170-years-ago/article24724665.ece.

8. "How Sugar Is Made—The History," https://www.sucrose.com/lhist.html.

9. "History of Sugar: Making Life Sweeter since 8000 BCE," https://www .sugar.org/sugar/history/; "Jaggery Sugar: An Ancient Indian Sweetener," *SPICEography* (blog), https://www.spiceography.com/jaggery-sugar/.

10. "Spiced Milk Tea (Masala Chai)," www.Epicurious.com, October 2009, https://www.epicurious.com/recipes/food/views/spiced-milk-tea-masala -chai-355421.

11. Lauren Frayer, "Hindu Nationalism, The Growing Trend in India," NPR, April 22, 2019, https://www.npr.org/2019/04/22/715875298/hindu-nationalism -the-growing-trend-in-india.

12. "India Job Data Spells Trouble for Narendra Modi," BBC, January 31, 2019, https://www.bbc.com/news/world-asia-india-47068223.

13. Lauren Frayer, "Black Lives Matter Gets Indians Talking about Skin Lightening

and Colorism," NPR, July 9, 2020, https://www.npr.org/sections/goatsand
soda/2020/07/09/860912124/black-lives-matter-gets-indians-talking-about
-skin-lightening-and-colorism.

14. Soutik Biswas, "Love Jihad: The Indian Law Threatening Interfaith Love,"
BBC, December 8, 2020, https://www.bbc.com/news/world-asia-india
-55158684.

15. "Cine Workers Association Writes to PM Modi, Demands Complete Shut-
down on Visa to Pakistani Actors," *India Today* (New Delhi), February 27, 2019,
https://www.indiatoday.in/movies/story/cine-workers-association-writes-Pm
-modi-demands-complete-shutdown-visa-pakistani-actors-1465906-2019-02-27.
When politically motivated cancellations and bans of Pakistani actors occur, it
is a huge loss for Bollywood.

16. Adrija Roychowdhury, "Naxalbari: How a Peasant Uprising Triggered a pan-
India Political Movement," *Indian Express*, May 25, 2018, https://indianexpress
.com/article/research/51-years-of-naxalbari-how-a-peasant-uprising-triggered
-a-pan-india-political-movement-5191046/.

17. "Confused between Maoists and Naxalites? Read On to Know the Difference,"
DNA, January 12, 2014, https://www.dnaindia.com/india/report-confused
-between-maoists-and-naxalities-read-on-to-know-the-difference-1949798.

18. Suvojit Bagchi, "Maoists Kill 15 in Chhattisgarh," *Hindu* (Raipur), March 11,
2014, updated June 8, 2016, https://www.thehindu.com/news/national/maoists
-kill-15-in-chhattisgarh/article5773315.ece.

19. Alok Pandey, "Actor-Activist Sadar Jafar Arrested for FB Live on Citizenship
Protest Gets Bail," NDTV, January 4, 2020, https://www.ndtv.com/india
-news/actor-activist-sadaf-jafar-arrested-in-up-for-doing-facebook-live-on
-citizenship-law-protest-gets-ba-2158768.

20. "Deadly Force Used against Protestors," Human Rights Watch, New York,
December 23, 2019, https://www.hrw.org/news/2019/12/23/india-deadly-force
-used-against-protesters.

21. "'Hum kaagaz nahin dikhayengey': Varun Grover's Anti-NRC Poem Wins
Support Online," *Indian Express* (New Delhi), December 23, 2019, https://
indianexpress.com/article/trending/trending-in-india/hum-kaagaz-nahi
-dikhayenge-varun-grovers-anti-nrc-poem-6179815/.

22. The translated lyrics can be found at https://snooplyrics.com/hum-kaagaz
-nahi-dikhayenge/. Grover has encouraged free use of this work globally.

23. Sam Levin and Nicky Woolf, "A Million People 'Check In' at Standing Rock
on Facebook to Support Dakota Pipeline Protestors," *Guardian* (US edition),

October 31, 2016, https://www.theguardian.com/us-news/2016/oct/31/north
-dakota-access-pipeline-protest-mass-facebook-check-in.

24. Kripa Krishnan, "A History Lesson about Iqbal Bano Who First Sang 'Hum
Dekhenge,'" iDiva.com, January 9, 2020, https://www.idiva.com/news-opinion
/news/a-history-lesson-about-iqbal-bano-who-first-sang-hum-dekhenge-in
-protest/18005737.

25. Ali Madeeh Hashmi, "When Iqbal Bano Defied Zia's Dictatorship to Sing
'Hum Dekhenge' at Alhamra," Naya Daur Media, September 4, 2019, https://
medium.com/@nayadaurpk/when-iqbal-bano-defied-zias-dictatorship-to-sing
-hum-dekheinge-at-alhamra-81f971eebe3d.

26. Mirza Arif Beg, "'Attacks Hindu Belief': IIT Kanpur Complainant on Faiz's
'Hum Dekhenge,'" Outlook, January 2, 2020, https://www.outlookindia.com
/website/story/hum-dekhenge-faizs-poem-that-went-from-rallying-cry-against
-caa-to-attack-on-hindu-belief/345029.

27. Prachi Verma, "Not Probing Faiz Poem but Student Protest: IIT Protest,"
Economic Times, January 3, 2020, https://economictimes.indiatimes.com/news
/politics-and-nation/not-probing-faiz-poem-but-student-protest-iit-kanpur
/articleshow/73077485.cms.

28. Elizabeth Puranan, "Why Shaheen Bagh Protests Are an Important Moment in
India's History," Al-Jazeera, February 3, 2020, https://www.aljazeera.com
/features/2020/2/3/why-shaheen-bagh-protests-are-an-important-moment
-in-indias-history.

29. Saritha S. Balan, "'Fight Is Not for Muslims Alone, but All Indians': Shaheen
Bagh Protester Asma Khatun," TheNEWSMinute, February 26, 2020, https://
www.thenewsminute.com/article/fight-not-muslims-alone-all-indians-shaheen
-bagh-protester-asma-khatun-119011.

30. Kai Schultz and Suhasini Raj, "Masked Men Attack Students in Rampage
at University in New Delhi," New York Times, January 5, 2020, https://www
.nytimes.com/2020/01/05/world/asia/india-jawaharlal-nehru-university-attack
.html.

31. "Old Lady React to Claims of Being Paid to Protest at Shaheen Bagh," YouTube,
https://www.youtube.com/watch?v=eRCGvoR73f4.

32. Ibid.

33. Somya Lakhani, "Explained: Who Is Bilkis, the Shaheen Bagh Dadi in TIME's
List of Most Influential People of 2020?," Indian Express, September 20, 2020,
https://indianexpress.com/article/explained/who-is-bilkis-the-shaheeb-bagh
-dadi-listed-among-times-most-influential-people-of-2020-6607454/.

34. Priya Ramani, "Adda and Lemon Tea at Shaheen Bagh," Live Mint, January 30,

2020, https://www.livemint.com/mint-lounge/features/adda-and-lemon-tea-at
-shaheen-bagh-11580364841235.html.

35. Instagram post for Cafe Temptation, Shaheen Bagh, Delhi, India, Novem-
ber 30, 2020, https://www.instagram.com/p/CIN_jX7nnza/; "The Best Time
Is Coffee Time," Instagram post for Café Temptation, Shaheen Bagh, Delhi,
India, November 3, 2019, https://www.instagram.com/p/B4agofGhTuA/; "Day
Should Start with Coffee & End with Ice-Cream," Instagram post for Café
Temptation, Shaheen Bagh, Delhi, India, November 30, 2020, https://www
.instagram.com/p/CIN_jX7nnza/.

36. Jeffrey Gettleman and Hari Kumar, "A Blow to the Head Makes an Instant
Hero in India," *New York Times*, January 17, 2020, https://www.nytimes.com/2020
/01/17/world/asia/india-protests-aishe-ghosh.html.

37. Sukrita Baruah, "At Shaheen Bagh, Graffiti Only Sign of Protest That Spread
across the Country," *Indian Express*, October 9, 2020, https://indianexpress.com
/article/cities/delhi/watching-sc-judgment-from-ground-zero-at-shaheen-bagh
-graffiti-only-sign-of-protest-6716599/.

38. "Padma Lakshmi: Taste the Nation, from Your Couch," *Ask Me Another*, NPR,
July 17, 2020, https://www.npr.org/2020/07/17/892239135/padma-lakshmi-taste
-the-nation-from-your-couch.

Chapter 9: Memory and What Makes a Family

1. "11 Important Facts You Should Know about Ravana," IndiaTV, October 16,
2015, https://www.indiatvnews.com/news/india/11-important-facts-you-should
-know-about-ravana-18313.html.

2. Dave Roos, "Why the 1918 Flu Pandemic Never Really Ended," History Channel, December 11, 2020, https://www.history.com/news/1918-flu-pandemic-never
-ended.

Chapter 10: The Rituals of the Great Pause

1. Phillippa Lally, Cornelia H. M. Van Jaarsveld, Henry W. W. Potts, and Jane
Wardle, "How Are Habits Formed: Modelling Habit Formation in the Real
World," *European Journal of Sociology and Psychology* 40, no. 6 (October 2010):
998–1009, https://doi.org/10.1002/ejsp.674.

2. Maxwell Maltz, *Psycho-Cybernetics Deluxe Edition: The Original Text of the Classic
Guide to a New Life* (TarcherPerigree, 016), 8.

3. "First Travel-Related Case of 2019 Novel Coronavirus Detected in United
States," Centers for Disease Control and Prevention, January 21, 2020, https://
www.cdc.gov/media/releases/2020/p0121-novel-coronavirus-travel-case.html.

4. Centers for Disease Control and Prevention, "Evidence for Limited Early Spread of COVID-19 within the United States, January–February 2020," Morbidity and Mortality Weekly Report, *Weekly* 69, no. 22 (June 5, 2020): 680–84, https://www.cdc.gov/mmwr/volumes/69/wr/mm6922e1.htm.

5. "A Timeline of COVID-19 Developments in 2020," *America Journal of Managed Care (AJMC)*, January 1, 2021, https://www.ajmc.com/view/a-timeline-of-covid19-developments-in-2020.

6. Unpublished interview, Nik Sharma and Madhushree Ghosh, January 11, 2021. See also "To Unlock Sublime Flavor, Cook like a Scientist," *Short Wave*, NPR, December 14, 2020, https://www.npr.org/transcripts/945611508. Emily Kwong and Rebecca Ramirez in conversation with Nik Sharma, author of *The Flavor Equation: The Science of Great Cooking Explained* (San Francisco: Chronicle Books, 2020).

7. Mayukh Sen, "An Indian Food Writer Breaks Free from Tradition," *New York Times*, October 2, 2018, https://www.nytimes.com/2018/10/02/dining/nik-sharma-season-cookbook.html.

8. Carlos C. Olaechea, "Is Rooh Afza the Most Refreshing Drink in the World?," *Food52* (blog), May 2020, https://food52.com/blog/24003-rooh-afza-summer-drink-of-the-east.

9. Emily VanDerWerff, "How to Bake Bread," *Vox*, May 19, 2020, https://www.vox.com/the-highlight/2020/5/19/21221008/how-to-bake-bread-pandemic-yeast-flour-baking-ken-forkish-claire-saffitz.

10. Elizabeth G. Dunn, "When Bakers Demanded More Flour, King Arthur Went to the Mills," *Bloomberg Businessweek*, June 16, 2020, https://www.bloomberg.com/news/features/2020-06-16/how-king-arthur-dealt-with-a-flour-shortage-during-the-pandemic.

11. "Our History: Two Centuries of Baking," King Arthur Baking Company, https://www.kingarthurbaking.com/about/history.

12. "Maneet Chauhan Bio," Food Network, https://www.foodnetwork.com/profiles/talent/maneet-chauhan/bio.

13. D. T. Hang and T. R. Preston, "Effect of Processing Taro Leaves on Oxalate Concentrations and Using the Ensiled Leaves as a Protein Source in Pig Diets in Central Vietnam," *Livestock Research for Rural Development* 22, no. 68 (2010), http://www.lrrd.org/lrrd22/4/hang22068.htm.

14. "Cauliflower Parmesan Pakoras with Sriracha," Nik Sharma (blog), November 1, 2014, http://abrowntable.com/home/cauliflower-parmesan-pakoras.

FOODSTORY

Nina Mukerjee Furstenau, series editor

Green Chili and Other Impostors
by Nina Mukerjee Furstenau

Khabaar:
An Immigrant Journey of Food, Memory, and Family
by Madhushree Ghosh